Against
the
Anthropocene

Against the Anthropocene

Visual Culture and Environment Today

T. J. Demos

Sternberg Press

Table of Contents

Chapter One

Welcome to the Anthropocene!

In a single lifetime we have grown into a phenomenal global force. We move more sediment and rock annually than all natural processes such as erosion and rivers. We manage three quarters of all land outside the ice sheets. Greenhouse gas levels this high have not been seen for over one million years. Temperatures are increasing. We have made a hole in the ozone layer. We are losing biodiversity. Many of the world's deltas are sinking due to damming, mining, and other causes. Sea level is rising. Ocean acidification is a real threat. We are altering Earth's natural cycles. We have entered the Anthropocene, a new geological epoch dominated by humanity.
—Globaïa, *Welcome to the Anthropocene*[1]

So explains the voice-over of the video *Welcome to the Anthropocene*, hosted on a website that claims to be the "world's first educational

1 Globaïa, *Welcome to the Anthropocene*, 2012, digital video, 3:28, from the website *Welcome to the Anthropocene*, accessed September 9, 2016, http://www.anthropocene.info /short-films.php.

Web portal on the Anthropocene," one dedicated to popularizing scientific discourse. Developed and sponsored by an international group of research organizations, the video was commissioned by the 2012 "Planet Under Pressure" conference that occurred in London.[2] Through its PR-style promotional media, we learn that we are now in a new geological epoch, the kind normally measured in millions of years. If we look further into what this era is and how it is defined, it turns out that, for some scientists, the period commenced more than two hundred years ago with the beginning of the industrial revolution, while, according to others, its origins stretch back twelve thousand years to the dawn of human agriculture. Some researchers, searching for definitive global shifts in the fossil record, suggest it coincides with the nuclear era, while still others argue that it began in 1492 with the arrival of Europeans in the Americas, initiating a massive rearrangement of life on earth. According to this latter scenario, the connection of the two hemispheres inaugurated the modern capitalist world system, founded upon imperial conquest, slavery, and much suffering and death. With the enormous loss of human life in the New World—from fifty-four million in 1492 to about six million in 1610—came massive reforestation and consequent carbon uptake by vegetation and soils, defining a major geological event measurable in the stratigraphic record, known as the "Orbis spike."[3] If that explanation is correct, we, as the video voice-over tells us, then "entered the Anthropocene, a new geological epoch dominated by humanity."

Notwithstanding the fact that this geological designation still awaits official confirmation of its boundaries by the Subcommission on Quaternary Stratigraphy's Working Group on the

---

2   *Welcome to the Anthropocene*, accessed June 9, 2016, http://www.anthropocene.info/. The network of sponsors includes: the International Geosphere-Biosphere Programme, Stockholm Resilience Centre of Stockholm University, Australia's Commonwealth Scientific and Industrial Research Organisation, the International Human Dimensions Programme on Global Environmental Change, and the Quebec nonprofit organization Globaïa.

3   Simon Lewis and Mark Maslin, "Defining the Anthropocene," *Nature* 519, no. 7542 (March 12, 2015): 174–75.

Anthropocene,[4] we might pause to ask: How does this new epoch—if it is indeed granted epoch status—and its discursive framework relate to image technologies, including the photographic, the video-based, the satellite-imaged, the website-delivered, and the network-dispersed? How is the Anthropocene thesis—for it remains for now a proposition that demands critical testing—abetted or contradicted by different kinds of visualizations, and how might artistic-activist practices not only confirm but also provide compelling alternatives to adopting its rhetoric? These questions will be addressed in this book, which, coming from a visual-cultural perspective grounded in the environmental arts and humanities, ultimately disputes the adoption of the Anthropocene as a legitimate term, offers reasoning as to why we should oppose it—in both theory and practice—and proposes alternatives in its place.

As explained by the partners of the popular science project Welcome to the Anthropocene (one of many now dedicated to publicizing the concept, according to diverse purposes and agendas), the term "Anthropocene" was introduced by atmospheric chemist Paul Crutzen and biologist Eugene Stoermer in 2000 to designate the present era, which for them has overtaken the Holocene that has been in existence for the last 11,700 years.[5] In fact,

4   In fact the Working Group recently voted in favor of adopting the Anthropocene as a term for our present, and will now seek to define its beginning point, not by date but by a specific boundary between layers of rock. This should take several years. According to reports, the Working Group is seriously considering the boundary of 1950, with the beginning of the nuclear age and radioactive elements dispersed across the planet by bomb tests, providing a global and historically specific geological signal. See Damian Carrington, "The Anthropocene Epoch: Scientists Declare Dawn of Human-Influenced Age," *Guardian*, August 29, 2016, https://www.theguardian.com/environment/2016/aug/29/declare-anthropocene-epoch-experts-urge-geological-congress-human-impact-earth.

5   By now there is an extensive introductory literature on the Anthropocene, among which are the following notable contributions: Frank Biermann, *Earth System Governance: World Politics in the Anthropocene* (Cambridge, MA: MIT Press, 2014); Katherine Gibson, Deborah Bird Rose, and Ruth Fincher, eds., *Manifesto for Living in the Anthropocene* (Brooklyn: Punctum Books, 2015); Christian Schwägerl, *The Anthropocene: The Human Era and How It Shapes Our Planet*, trans. Lucy Renner Jones (Santa Fe: Synergetic Press, 2014); Joanna Zylinska, *Minimal Ethics for the Anthropocene* (London: Open Humanities Press, 2014); Gaia Vince,

geologists have entertained this and similar terms since the mid-nineteenth century, when the Welsh geologist Thomas Jenkyn proposed the "Anthropozoic" for the current "human epoch," reprised by Reverend William Houghton in 1865. The first use of "the Anthropocene" appears to be in 1922, by the Russian geologist Aleksei Pavlov to designate the present "Anthropogenic system (period) or Anthropocene."[6] That terminological genealogy notwithstanding, the shift in Earth's systems, we are told repeatedly in the recent literature and in the science media, owes to "human activities," which have allegedly become the central drivers of the geologically significant conditions in our present.[7] The changes include biogeochemical alterations to the composition of the atmosphere, oceans, and soils, bringing about many destructive ecological transformations such as global warming, ocean acidification, expanding oceanic dead zones, and increased species extinction owing to habitat loss and environmental destruction, transformations that are at the forefront of current ecological and political debates concerned with how to mitigate and/or adapt to their impacts. As theorist McKenzie Wark observes, we have entered the "end of pre-history," a time when "the worldview of an ecology that was self-correcting, self-balancing and self-healing—is dead."[8] We now live in a time of "metabolic rift," according to Wark's invocation of Karl Marx's prescient writing on political ecology, when environmental matters, from molecules to water cycles, weather patterns to climates, are out of joint.[9]

Adventures in the Anthropocene: A Journey to the Heart of the Planet We Made (London: Chatto & Windus, 2014); and Clive Hamilton, Christophe Bonneuil, and François Gemenne, eds., *The Anthropocene and the Global Environmental Crisis: Rethinking Modernity in a New Epoch* (Abingdon: Routledge, 2015).

6   Lewis and Maslin, "Defining the Anthropocene," 172–73.

7   "Glossary," *Welcome to the Anthropocene*, accessed August 17, 2016, http://www.anthropocene.info/en/glossary.

8   McKenzie Wark, *Molecular Red: Theory for the Anthropocene* (London: Verso, 2015), 14.

9   For a useful analysis of Marx's notion of metabolic rift, see John Bellamy Foster, *Marx's Ecology: Materialism and Nature* (New York: Monthly Review Press, 2000).

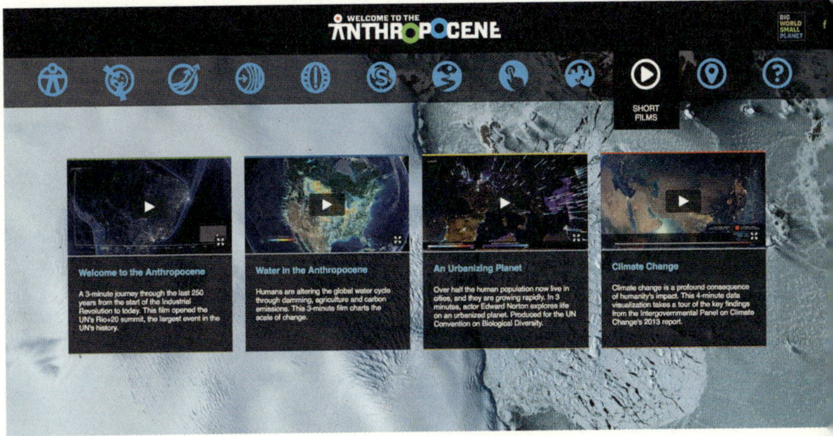

Screenshot of the website Welcome to the Anthropocene*, October 2016*

Recently broached in the natural sciences and propelled further in popular science educational media, the Anthropocene has also become part of an expanding discourse in the arts, humanities, and social sciences, debated by figures like Bruno Latour, Eduardo Viveiros de Castro, Donna Haraway, and Anna Tsing, and taken up in new scholarly journals, such as *The Anthropocene*, *The Anthropocene Review*, and *Elementa*. The trend is present in cultural practices, art exhibitions, and catalogue publications, such as the "Anthropocene Project" at the Haus der Kulturen der Welt in Berlin (2013–15) and the recent compilation volume *Art in the Anthropocene: Encounters among Aesthetics, Politics, Environments and Epistemologies* (2015), edited by Heather Davis and Etienne Turpin. These contributions—more on which later— alone make the Anthropocene worthy of our attention, particularly for those of us working in the cultural realm, but especially as they point to a massive transformation that is occurring in how we might comprehend the present intersection of human culture and the environment that is remaking the world as we know it. It remains urgent to bring these critical humanities- and arts- based resources to bear on scientific discourse in order to disrupt specialist divisions, democratize debate, and pose critical questions of political significance to discussions on environmental developments. For in one way or another they are having major, if differentiated, impact on the lives of all. A good starting point is to ask: How does the Anthropocene enter into visuality, and what are its politics of representation?

Welcome to the Anthropocene offers an authoritative voice-over commentary that narrates shifting data visualizations of the globe, showing schematic networks of light trajectories that reference and measure energy, transportation, and communication systems. The same visual information is presented on the "Cartography of the Anthropocene" webpage,[10] produced by Globaïa, one of the organizations responsible for the website *Welcome to the Anthropocene*, and "dedicated to fostering awareness among citizens by promoting the emergence of a global vision of our world and of the great socioecological challenges of our time."[11] The page offers a series of images with various representational modalities, showing cities, global shipping and air transportation routes, pipeline networks, and submarine fiber-optic cable systems, as well as the growth of carbon dioxide pollution over the last few centuries. The presentation charts the interconnected networks of so-called human activities that visualize how, according to the voice-over, "we have grown into a phenomenal global force," even while many humans would certainly resist identifying with the collective "we" of the implied Anthropocene subject, with its proposed universally distributed responsibility for the causes of the climate change it names.

Such imagery additionally speaks to a problem articulated by recent theorists of ecology: that the expanded spatial and temporal scales of geology exceed human comprehension, and thereby

10   "Cartography of the Anthropocene," *Globaïa*, accessed September 22, 2016, http://globaia
       .org/portfolio/cartography-of-the-anthropocene/.
11   "Mission and Goals," *Globaïa*, accessed September 22, 2016, http://globaia.org/about
       /mission/.

present major challenges to representational systems.[12] For once we start talking about the massively distributed and temporally extended "hyperobjects" of geology, to use Timothy Morton's term, the minute-by-comparison pictorial conventions of land-scape photography—even those of photography at large—suddenly become far from adequate. The environmental humanities scholar Rob Nixon articulates the political dimensions and policy-related implications of this challenge: "A central question is stra-tegic and representational: How can we convert into image and narrative the disasters that are slow moving and long in the mak-ing, disasters that are anonymous and that star nobody, disasters that are attritional and of indifferent interest to the sensation-driven technologies of our image-world? How can we turn the long emergencies of slow violence into stories dramatic enough to rouse public sentiment and warrant political interventions, these emer-gencies whose repercussions have given rise to some of the most critical challenges of our time?"[13]

Anthropocene visualizations, which seldom focus on environ-mental emergencies and attritional scenes of slow violence, introduce an added complexity in that they often do not employ photography as their visual medium of choice, but rather opt for high-resolution sat-ellite imagery that provides photographic-like pictures, such as those employed by Globaïa. That is important insofar as—at least in rela-tion to much scientifically framed imagery, maps, and data graphs—we have moved essentially beyond photography (historically and conventionally gauged to human perception) to remote sensing tech-nology (scaled to global, even interplanetary measurements). Seem-ingly existing as self-evident pictures, satnav imagery resembles

---

12   See Timothy Morton, *Hyperobjects: Philosophy and Ecology after the End of the World* (Min-neapolis: University of Minnesota Press, 2013); and Elizabeth Ellsworth and Jamie Kruse, eds., *Making the Geologic Now: Responses to Material Conditions of Contemporary Life* (Brooklyn: Punctum Books, 2012).

13   Rob Nixon, *Slow Violence and the Environmentalism of the Poor* (Cambridge, MA: Harvard University Press, 2011), 3.

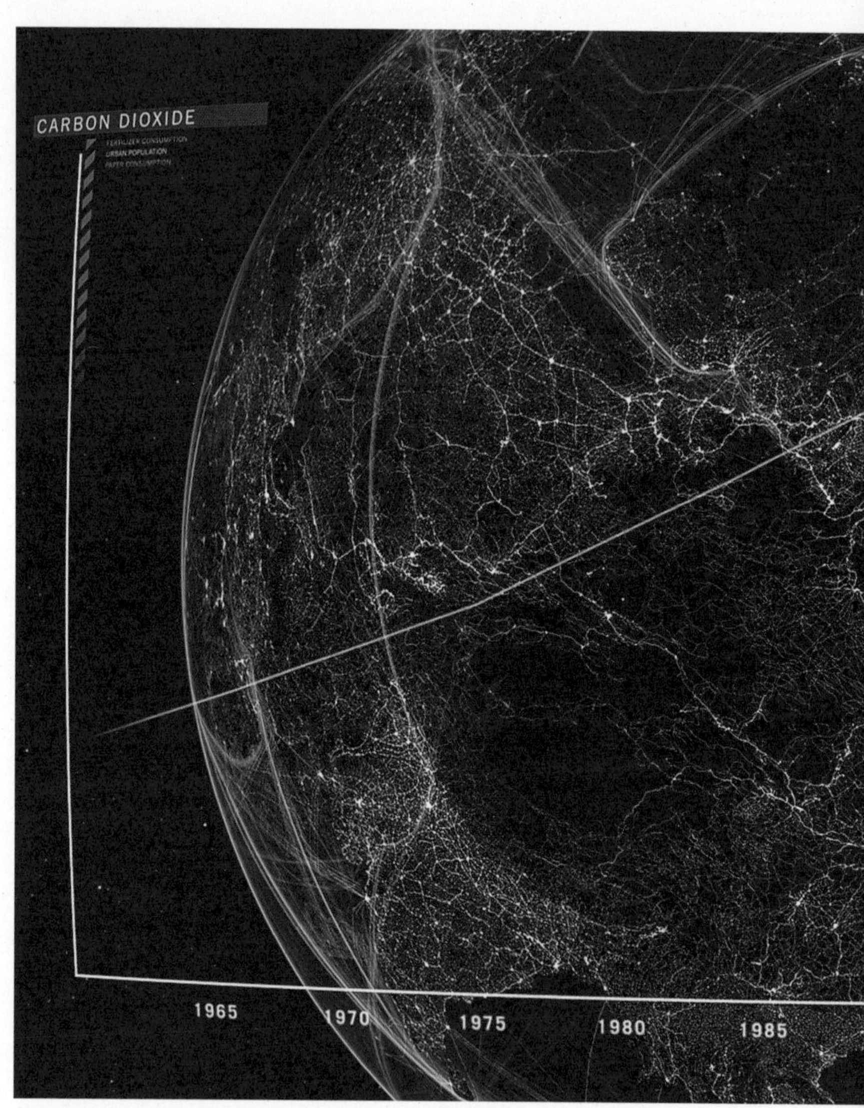
CARBON DIOXIDE
FERTILIZER CONSUMPTION
URBAN POPULATION
PAPER CONSUMPTION
1965
1970
1975
1980
1985

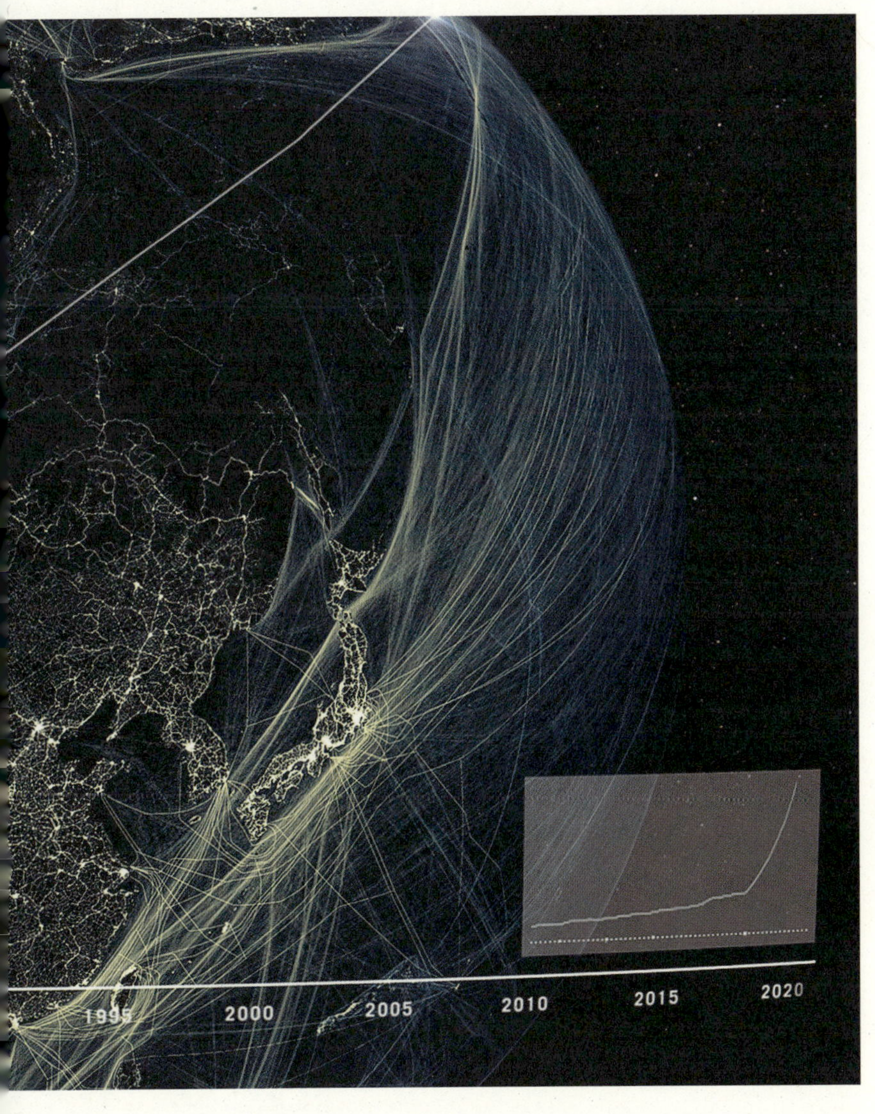

Still from Globaïa's video *Welcome to the Anthropocene*, 2012; documenting the acceleration in human activity since the industrial revolution

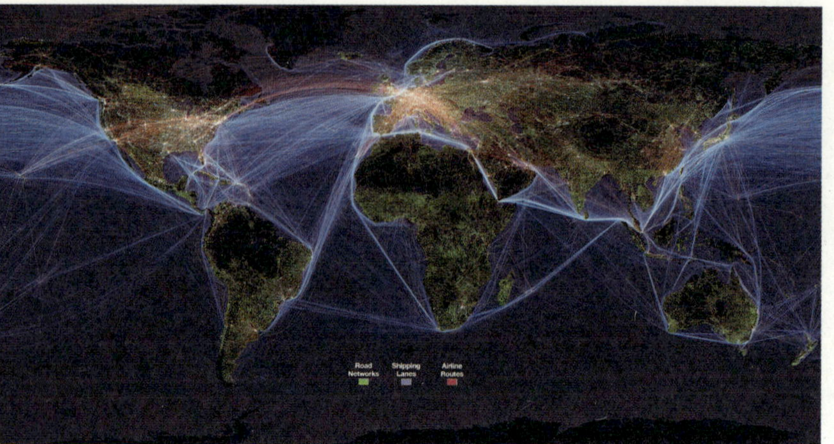

Global Transportation System map from Globaïa's webpage "Cartography of the Anthropocene," October 2016

and is often taken for photography, but actually comprises a composite set of digitized files, the result of processed quantities of data collected by satellite-based sensors, much of it invisible to human perception. For architecture theorist and director of the Spatial Information Design Lab, Laura Kurgan, such imagery symptomatizes "a cataclysmic shift in our ability to navigate, inhabit, and define the spatial realm [...] brought on by: the operationalizing of Global Positioning System (GPS) satellites for both military and civilian uses in 1991; the democratization and distribution of data and imagery on the World Wide Web in 1992; the proliferation of desktop computing and the use of geographic information systems for the management of data; the privatization of commercial high-resolution satellites later in the 1990s; and widespread mapping made possible by Google Earth in 2005."[14] This shift has effectively made possible the entrance into visuality of the Anthropocene—indeed, such representational technology is integral to the "vast machine" that is the "sociotechnical system that collects data, models physical processes,

14   Laura Kurgan, *Close Up at a Distance: Mapping, Technology and Politics* (Brooklyn: Zone Books, 2014), 14.

tests theories, and ultimately generates a widely shared understanding of climate and climate change."[15] Yet in most cases regarding lay usage, these images have not only been carefully edited in order to show generally positive examples of modern development, but they have also already been interpreted for viewers (or rather consumers), insofar as they have been packaged as pictures, but without typically offering access to location data, ownership, legibility, or source information.[16] In other words, the images seem hyper-legible, but in fact they are far from transparent or direct.

While visual imagery has been central, even integral to the process of conceptualizing the Anthropocene, scientific popularizers rarely evince awareness of, let alone educate their audience regarding, the use of such imagery. Nor do they typically address the implications of their representations, which not only help illustrate geological concepts, but also frame them in particular ways that are deeply political, though infrequently presented or acknowledged as such. As well, those images bear the potential to be read differently, potentially contesting and complicating some of Anthropocene theory's basic claims—if analyzed critically.[17]

As indicated above, one initial problem with the term "Anthropocene" lies at the very root of the term: *anthropos*, ancient Greek for "man" or "human being." Etymologically, the term's root secures

---

15   Paul N. Edwards, *A Vast Machine: Computer Models, Climate Data, and the Politics of Global Warming* (Cambridge, MA: MIT Press, 2010), 8.

16   Globaïa, however, does provide the following note on its use of data, which nevertheless, only seems to make the image more opaque: "DATA SOURCE: Paved and Unpaved Roads, Pipelines, Railways & Transmission Lines: VMap0, National Geospatial-Intelligence Agency, September 2000. Shipping Lanes: NOAA's SEAS BBXX database, from 14.10.2004 to 15.10.2005. Air Networks: International Civil Aviation Organization statistics. Urban Areas: naturalearthdata.com. Submarine Cables: Greg Mahlknecht's Cable Map. Earth texture maps: Tom Patterson. Anthropocene Indicators: *Global Change and the Earth System: A Planet Under Pressure*, Steffen, W., Sanderson, A., Jäger, J., Tyson, P. D., Moore III, B., Matson, P. A., Richardson, K., Oldfield, F., Schellnhuber, H.-J., Turner II, B. L., Wasson, R. J.," in "Cartography of the Anthropocene," *Globaïa*, accessed September 9, 2016, http://globaia.org/portfolio/cartography-of-the-anthropocene/.

17   In this regard, with new imaging technologies, we need to cultivate new ways of seeing. A recent primer on this task, which insists on interlinking vision with political insight, is

the concept of "human activities" that are ostensibly responsible for this new geological epoch. Indeed, the formulation is commonly found in the literature, including the *Welcome to the Anthropocene* website, the video *Welcome to the Anthropocene*, and Crutzen and Stoermer's 2000 essay that is often cited as the catalyst for setting the current Anthropocene debate in motion.[18] Yet the "activities" that are shown in the imagery that commonly depicts said epoch are hardly "human," at least in that generalizing, species-being sense, but are in fact mostly the "activities" of corporate industry, an area generally occluded in Anthropocene discourse. This simple fact leads us to ask: What ideological function does the word "Anthropocene" serve—terminologically as well as conceptually, politically, and visually—in relation to the current politics of ecology, and how does the expanded imagery of what was once "photography" abet or complicate this function?

As is well understood by critics, the data visualization tools used by the Globaïa website, like Google Earth mapping imagery more generally, is embedded in a specific political and economic framework, comprising a visual system delivered and constituted by the post-Cold War and largely Western-based military-state-corporate apparatus. It offers an innocent-seeming picture that is in fact a "techno-scientific, militarized, 'objective' image."[19] (Interestingly, Crutzen cut his teeth as a scientist in the Cold War context during the 1980s, taking the earth to be a theater of large-

Nicholas Mirzoeff, *How to See the World: An Introduction to Images, from Self-Portraits to Selfies, Maps to Movies, and More* (New York: Basic Books, 2016).

18 Paul Crutzen and Eugene Stoermer, "The 'Anthropocene,'" *Global Change Newsletter* 41 (2000): 17. They write of the "major and still growing impacts of *human activities* on earth and the atmosphere, and at all, including global, scales," which make it "more than appropriate to emphasize the central role of mankind in geology and ecology by proposing to use the term 'anthropocene' for the current geological epoch" (my emphasis).

19 Kurgan, *Close Up at a Distance*, 30. Trevor Paglen also importantly points out that satellite imagery is "produced by and, in turn, productive of an enormous relational geography with political, economic, legal, social, and cultural aspects." Trevor Paglen, "IV. Geographies of Photography," *Still Searching* (blog), April 11, 2013, http://blog.fotomuseum.ch/2014/04/iv-geographies-of-photography/.

scale military intervention potentially transformed by a "nuclear winter" following nuclear war, an experience that fed into his consideration of geoengineering in the 1990s as a means of tackling climate change.)[20] It is worth asking to what degree the Anthropocene itself—as a discursive formation with legal, political, cultural, and geological strands—is a function of that system, despite its scientific terminological origins (a question to which I will return later). My argument, in brief, is that Anthropocene rhetoric—joining images and texts—frequently acts as a mechanism of universalization, albeit complexly mediated and distributed among various agents, which enables the military-state-corporate apparatus to disavow responsibility for the differentiated impacts of climate change, effectively obscuring the accountability behind the mounting eco-catastrophe and inadvertently making us all complicit in its destructive project.

This universalizing logic has a history. Images of the globe first circulated widely in 1968, when NASA made photographs available taken by its ATS-3 satellite a year earlier. Stewart Brand's *Whole Earth Catalog* published one of these, fulfilling its quest for an image of the globe (though Buckminster Fuller correctly pointed out at the time that the image is far from "whole" and in fact shows only half the planet).[21] In 1972, the famous "Blue Marble" photograph was taken. One of the most reproduced images in visual cultural history to date, the photo was shot by NASA astronauts with a seventy-millimeter Hasselblad camera aboard the Apollo 17 spacecraft. The image answered calls, as voiced by Brand and many oth-

---

20 See Christophe Bonneuil and Jean-Baptiste Fressoz, "Who Is the Anthropos?," in *The Shock of the Anthropocene: The Earth, History and Us*, trans. David Fernbach (London: Verso, 2016), 92.

21 Reported in an interview with Stewart Brand conducted by Joseph Corn (Buckminster Fuller Lectures, Stanford University, Stanford, CA, February 27, 2002), excerpts found here, accessed September 20, 2016: http://www.hohlwelt.com/en/interact/context/sbrand .html. On Fuller, see Felicity D. Scott, *Architecture or Techno-utopia: Politics after Modernism* (Cambridge, MA: MIT Press, 2007), 202.

ers, for a unifying "world perspective" that could bring earthlings together visually—and thus sociopolitically.[22] According to proponents, a visualization of the whole earth would facilitate a new era of global peace based on a shared planetary identity that would overcome the political, social, national, and other divisions then rocking the planet (including Cold War conflicts, the American war in Vietnam, United States–sponsored military dictatorships in Latin America, anticolonial struggle in Apartheid South Africa, sociopolitical upheavals in Europe and the United States, and tumultuous processes of decolonization in Africa and Asia). "If we are to have peace on Earth," intoned Martin Luther King Jr. in 1967, "we must develop a world perspective."[23]

King's "world perspective," approximated by the remarkable Apollo 17 image, indeed catalyzed hopes for unification, even though its view, shot from seemingly nowhere, also negates the specific agency of the image's creation. As such, one might equally argue that its universalizing image depended on an antipolitical excision of disagreement and conflict, the acknowledgment and negotiation of which is the fundamental condition of democracy.[24] As anthropologist Tim Ingold writes, "The significance of the image of the globe in the language of contemporary debate about the environment" is problematic precisely because it renders the world "as an object of contemplation detached from the domain of lived

22 For instance, Frank Borman, Apollo 8 mission commander, made the following comment upon seeing the first image of Earth from outer space taken in 1968: "When you're finally up at the moon looking back at the earth, all those differences and nationalistic traits are pretty well going to blend and you're going to get a concept that maybe this is really one world and why the hell can't we learn to live together like decent people?" Cited in Denis Cosgrove, *Apollo's Eye: A Cartographic Genealogy of the Earth in the Western Imagination* (Baltimore: Johns Hopkins University Press, 2001), 258. See also Diedrich Diederichsen and Anselm Franke, eds., *The Whole Earth: California and the Disappearance of the Outside* (Berlin: Sternberg Press, 2013).

23 Cited in Edward Rothstein, "A Mirror of Greatness, Blurred," *New York Times*, August 25, 2011, http://www.nytimes.com/2011/08/26/arts/design/martin-luther-king-jr-national-memorial-opens-in-washington.html?_r=0.

24 See, for instance, Chantal Mouffe, *On the Political* (London: Routledge, 2005), for whom politics is constituted by the agonistic dimension.

experience."[25] In other words, it is both an ideal image and an image of idealism, perfect for an antipolitical neo-humanist culture following upon the devastating divisions of two world wars.

While one might justifiably propose correlates of that situation to contemporary conditions, today, Anthropocene images tend to be directed in very different ways, foremost among them: to raise awareness of the "human activities" that have disrupted the earth's natural systems in our era of climate change. In addition, they are often used, as we shall see, to demonstrate the achievements and impacts of the human mastery of the planet via geoengineering, which is frequently pitched as our only remaining hope in adapting to inevitable environmental transformation, even as that conclusion is contested by activists who argue for "system change, not climate change."[26] Nonetheless, the Anthropocene, much like the preceding *Whole Earth* rhetoric, functions as a universalizing discourse: it tends to disavow differentiated responsibility (and the differently located effects) for the geological changes it designates, instead homogeneously allocating agency to the generic members of its "human activities." As such, it avoids the politicization of ecology that could otherwise lead to the practice of climate justice, which demands that the politics of equality, human rights, and historical responsibility be taken into account when addressing environmental change.[27]

25 Tim Ingold, "Globes and Spheres: The Topology of Environmentalism," in *Environmentalism: The View from Anthropology*, ed. Kay Milton (London: Routledge, 1993), 31–32.

26 See Clive Hamilton, *Earthmasters: The Dawn of the Age of Climate Engineering* (New Haven, CT: Yale University Press, 2014).

27 Such a tendency of avoidance is a longstanding operation of mainstream, corporate-supported environmentalism, as described in Finis Dunaway, *Seeing Green: The Use and Abuse of Environmental Images* (Chicago: University of Chicago Press, 2015). For an elaboration of the radical alternatives of political ecology, see the websites of Climate Justice Now! ("a network of organisations and movements from across the globe committed to the fight for social, ecological and gender justice"), accessed August 17, 2016, http://climatejustice now.org/; and System Change not Climate Change ("a joint Canadian and US coalition of ecosocialists and fellow travellers united in the belief that capitalism is driving climate change and that a radical international grassroots movement can stop it"), accessed August 17, 2016, http://systemchangenotclimatechange.org/.

How does that disavowal operate? How might it be challenged photographically or via photographic-like imagery? If the Anthropocene thesis anesthetizes politics, what would it mean to politicize its visual culture?

Welcome to the Anthropocene!

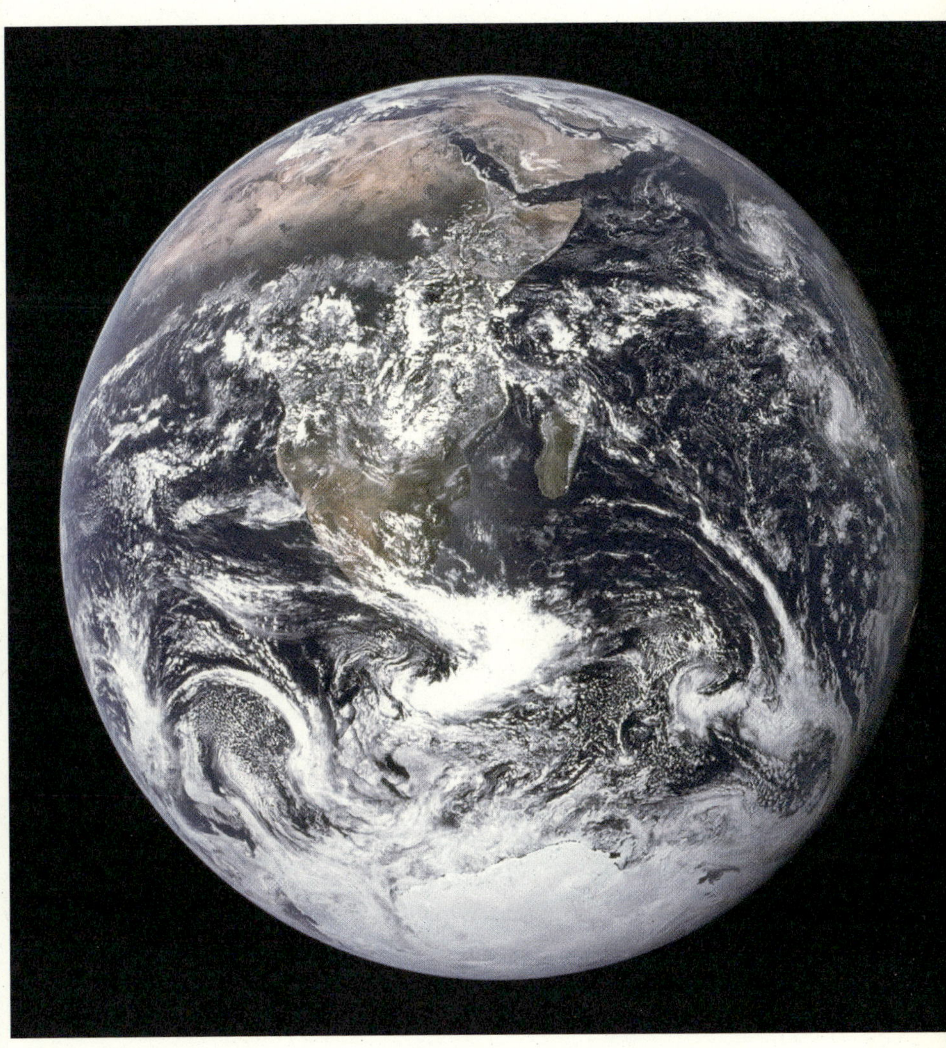

Earth as seen by the Apollo 17 crew, 1972

Chapter Two

Geoengineering the Anthropocene

> A daunting task lies ahead for scientists and engineers to guide society towards environmentally sustainable management during the era of the Anthropocene. This will require appropriate human behaviour at all scales, and may well involve internationally accepted, large-scale geo-engineering projects, for instance to "optimize" climate.
> —Paul J. Crutzen[1]

The Anthropocene thesis, as presented in an increasingly expanding body of images and texts, appears generally split between optimists and pessimists, especially when it comes to geoengineering, the deliberate intervention in the earth's natural systems to counteract the negative effects of climate change. As the Anthropocene appears to imply the necessity of geoengineering—as Crutzen makes clear in the quote above—the battle lines have been drawn between those who think "we" humans confront an extraordinary opportunity to

1   Paul J. Crutzen, "Geology of Mankind," *Nature* 415, no. 23 (January 3, 2002): 23.

biotechnologically remake the world, and others who opt for hands-off caution and would rather modify human behavior instead of the environment in addressing the climate crisis.

For instance, ethics philosopher Clive Hamilton, participating in "The Anthropocene: An Engineered Age?," a 2014 panel discussion at Berlin's Haus der Kulturen der Welt, broke the world down into techno-utopians and eco-Soterians. The former are today's "new Prometheans," intent on intervening in climate systems, even creating a new Eden on Earth; the latter, named after Soteria, the ancient Greek personification of safety and preservation, remain pledged to the precautionary principle—the principle that states "where there are threats of serious or irreversible damage, lack of full scientific certainty shall not be used as a reason for postponing cost-effective measures to prevent environmental degradation."[2] Eco-Soterians prioritize respect for the earth's processes and remain critical of human hubris, the very same hubris, they argue, that got us into the environmental crisis in the first place.[3] For sociologist Bruno Latour, leaning toward the optimistic side of the scale, we must not disown what he calls the "contemporary Frankenstein" we have created—the earth of the Anthropocene—but rather learn to love and care for the "monster" we have created.[4] Meanwhile, for

2   "Rio Declaration on Environment and Development" (1992), *United Nations Environment Programme*, accessed June 9, 2016, http://www.unep.org/Documents.multilingual/Default.asp?DocumentID=78&ArticleID=1163&l=en (page discontinued).

3   See the recording of "The Anthropocene: An Engineered Age?" (panel discussion, Haus der Kulturen der Welt, Berlin, August 21, 2014), including:Bernd M. Scherer (director, Haus der Kulturen der Welt); Mark Lawrence (IASS-Potsdam); Klaus Töpfer (IASS-Potsdam); Armin Grunwald (Office of Technology Assessment of the German Parliament); Clive Hamilton (Charles Sturt University); and Thomas Ackerman (University of Washington), moderated by Oliver Morton (*Economist*), YouTube video, 1:54:12, posted by "IASS Potsdam," August 28, 2014, https://www.youtube.com/watch?v=C9huFiOo3qk. Notable techno-utopian contributions include: Mark Lynas, *The God Species: Saving the Planet in the Age of Humans* (London: Fourth Estate, 2011); and David W. Keith, *A Case for Climate Engineering* (Cambridge, MA: MIT Press, 2013).

4   Bruno Latour, "Love Your Monsters: Why We Must Care for Our Technologies as We Do Our Children," *Breakthrough* 2 (Winter 2012), http://thebreakthrough.org/index.php0/journal/past-issues/issue-2/love-your-monsters.

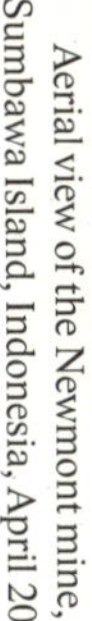

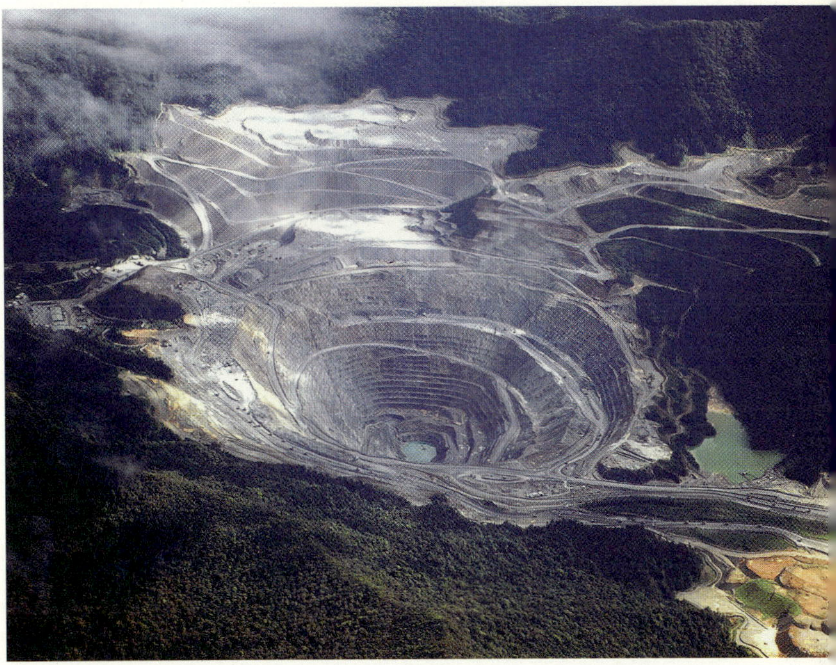

Aerial view of the Newmont mine, Sumbawa Island, Indonesia, April 2007

activist Naomi Klein, on the opposite side, arguments like Latour's are dangerously misguided: "The earth is not our prisoner, our patient, our machine, or, indeed, our monster. It is our entire world. And the solution to global warming is not to fix the world, it is to fix ourselves."[5]

In fact the visual culture of the Anthropocene, whether delivered photographically or via remote-sensing technology, is riven by exactly this tension. As with images of the giant Newmont mine on Sumbawa Island in Indonesia, which is visible from outer space, Anthropocene iconography both portrays the remarkable extent of the human-driven alteration of earth systems (with ample

5   Naomi Klein, *This Changes Everything: Capitalism vs. the Climate* (New York: Allen Lane, 2014), 279.

photographic and satellite-based imagery of large-scale mining, oil drilling, infrastructure, and deforestation projects), and documents the dangers of the unintended consequences of such ventures. Ultimately, however, imaging systems play more than an illustrative role here, as they tend to grant viewers a sense of control over the represented object of their gaze, even if that control is far from reality.

In other words, Anthropocene visuality tends to reinforce the techno-utopian position that "we" have indeed mastered nature, just as we have mastered its imaging—and in fact the two, the dual colonization of nature and representation, appear inextricably intertwined.[6] In this sense, representation merges with neo-Promethean engineering and science: the Anthropocene places technocrats and scientists in the role of bringing about a great awakening regarding climate change and then conveniently puts those same figures in the position of being the only ones that can fix the problem—via geoengineering.[7] Yet geoengineering projects are invented and proposed generally by large corporations, heavy industry, and well-resourced nations, and supported, not surprisingly, by the likes of Microsoft mogul and philanthropist Bill Gates.[8] None of them is quite identical to the abstract "human" subject of the Anthropocene, a distinction that potentially pushes the neologism to its breaking point. That many nonetheless tend to identify with the Anthropocene thesis, including its generalizations, universalizations, and geoengineering ideology, is part of its

6   For further discussion of cultural practices that seek to provide creative alternatives to this system, see T. J. Demos, *Decolonizing Nature: Contemporary Art and the Politics of Ecology* (Berlin: Sternberg Press, 2016).

7   As Bonneuil and Fressoz point out, in "Who Is the Anthropos?," 76.

8   See John Vidal, "Bill Gates Backs Climate Scientists Lobbying for Large-Scale Geoengineering," *Guardian*, February 6, 2012, https://www.theguardian.com/environment/2012/feb/06/bill-gates-climate-scientists-geoengineering. For a report on the forthcoming large-scale Harvard geoengineering experiment, the first of its kind conducted in Earth's atmosphere, see: Arthur Neslen, "US scientists launch world's biggest solar geoengineering study," *Guardian*, March 24, 2017, https://www.theguardian.com/environment/2017/mar/24/us-scientists-launch-worlds-biggest-solar-geoengineering-study.

very "conspiracy," in the terms of Etienne Turpin, who condemns the willing collusion, the thoughtless enrollment of cooperation, with the Anthropocene's principles, rather than the critical interrogation of its fundamental terms.[9]

That said, critics and commentators (including those taking part in "The Anthropocene: An Engineered Age?" panel discussion), have posed important questions about the ethical implications of Anthropocene geoengineering, including: Should humans undertake such projects—like solar radiation management (spraying fine sea water to whiten clouds in the troposphere, or applying stratospheric sulfate aerosols to reflect sunlight to combat warming), or carbon capture technologies to lower greenhouse gases in the atmosphere—when they acknowledge that massive geologically interventionist processes will inevitably involve unforeseen consequences and unanticipated effects? If reducing sun exposure in the northern hemisphere may unintentionally bring irregular or extreme monsoons in India and Bangladesh, then how will such eventualities be negotiated, especially given unequal global power relations and the lack of international environmental governance protocol?

We could add still more thorny questions (notwithstanding the central one of whether or not such technologies will even work): What system of ethics governs the use of such technology? Who has the right—which individuals, governments, or corporations— to conduct these experiments, and who will pay the costs when accidents occur? And if rights generally derive from nation-states, then what legitimate body can grant permission to geoengineering projects operating on a global scale? These are all serious queries that await answers, and they again raise the specters of geopolitical inequalities and disproportionate causes and effects of climate

9   As expressed in Etienne Turpin's presentation, "Conspiracies of the Anthropocene" (Arts in Society Conference, Los Angeles, August 11, 2016, where I presented an early version of *Against the Anthropocene*).

change that the term Anthropocene fails to indicate or contain.[10] In this sense, the "Anthropocenologists," as Christophe Bonneuil and Jean-Baptiste Fressoz pejoratively refer to adherents, have effectively created a "state of exception": "They manufacture a global nature-system that is no longer a commons regulated by collective debate, practices and rights, but one whose exclusive access is strictly regulated as a function of the rights, subject to emergency circumstances, to alter, pilot and optimize the whole of the planet and its atmosphere."[11] The problem is that the "exclusive access" to those rights is held by a select minority, a situation that mirrors increasing forms of global economic and sociopolitical inequality, and illiberal governance.

Consider the case of rogue American entrepreneur Russ George, who released around one hundred tons of iron sulfate into the Pacific Ocean off the west coast of Canada in 2012 to catalyze an artificial plankton bloom as large as four thousand square miles. The goal of this pet geoengineering experiment—the largest of its kind worldwide to date—was to test the absorption of carbon dioxide by plankton who will then, according to the anticipated scenario, sink to the ocean floor, a sequestration procedure and "ecosystem service" still in development from which George, CEO of Planktos Inc., hopes to massively profit.[12] In the process of conducting his trial run, he transgressed various international agreements, including the United Nations convention on biological diversity, and violated the trust of the Haida First Nations people who, allegedly deceived by George, regrettably approved the project in advance.[13]

---

10   For the beginning of a consideration of these questions, see Biermann, *Earth System Governance*, which calls for new mechanisms and institutions to develop environmental governance, such as a revitalized United Nations, and the establishment of a World Environment Organization.

11   Bonneuil and Fressoz, "Who Is the Anthropos?," 92–93.

12   See *Planktos Ecosystems*, accessed September 20, 2016, http://www.planktos.com/.

13   See Martin Lukacs, "World's Biggest Geoengineering Experiment 'Violates' UN Rules," *Guardian*, October 15, 2012, https://www.theguardian.com/environment/2012/oct/15/pacific-iron-fertilisation-geoengineering. Lukacs also reports that "scientists are debating

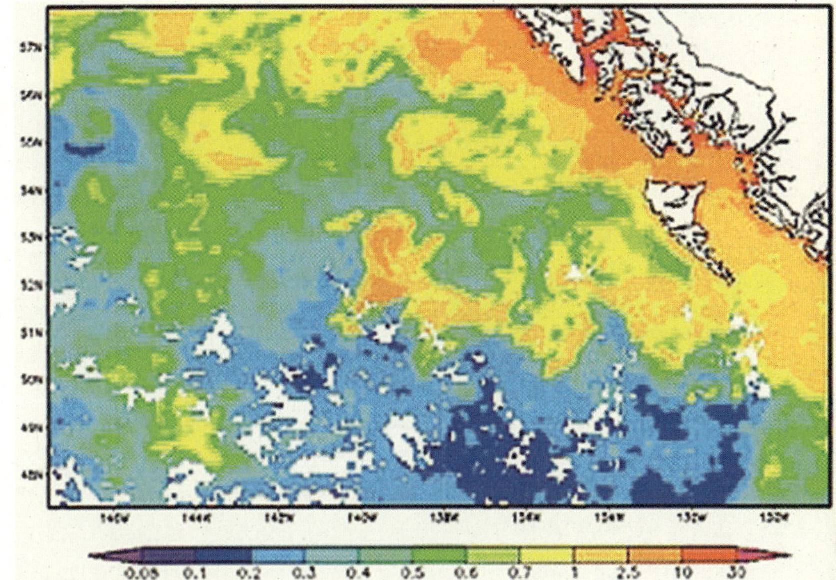

The yellow and orange colors in the center of this graph, produced by NASA in August 2012, reveal unnaturally high levels of chlorophyll off the coast of British Columbia after Russ George's geoengineering scheme.

Aside from the still-unresolved assessment of the success or failure of the experiment, which may stand to irreparably harm ocean ecosystems, the case exemplifies how, with the Anthropocene, we confront a completely unregulated project, following from the impossibility of representing—politically as much as institutionally—the global citizenry (including regional bodies) that should be, and have every right to be, participants in current discussions of how our world is shaped. In other words, the Anthropocene has no system of democratic governance.

While the 2014 panel "The Anthropocene: An Engineered Age?" also addressed the Anthropocene's democratic deficit, supporting the need for more inclusive debate when it comes to geoengineering—with which one can only agree—it was telling that the

whether iron fertilisation can lock carbon into the deep ocean over the long term, and have raised concerns that it can irreparably harm ocean ecosystems, produce toxic tides and lifeless waters, and worsen ocean acidification and global warming."

panel was composed solely of white European and North American men of science, glimpsing, despite words to the contrary, exactly the kind of technocracy that is the elite and exclusive governance structure of our current geological epoch.[14] The way that governance structure operates, and by extension how it might address the risks of future geoengineering, can be predicted, no doubt, on the basis of recent industrial (mal)practice, which characteristically is recklessly accident-prone, exclusively profit-driven, and largely devoid of democratic accountability. In order to better understand the near future of the geoengineered Anthropocene, we can look to the recent past.

Take the infamous 2010 BP Deepwater Horizon oil spill disaster in the Gulf of Mexico, an eco-catastrophe that is all-too-quickly receding in the public sphere's short-term attention span, as it is historically buried by subsequent climate change disasters and industrial accidents. The explosion and consequent fire on the oil platform generated a slew of spectacular images of the industrial-apocalyptic sublime, including those of the blazing plume attended by fireboat response crews dousing the inferno with water. Other shots depicted charismatic sea animals pathetically covered in black goo resulting from the release of approximately 260 million gallons of crude into the gulf's waters (untold numbers have died and will die from the spill's slow violence unfolding for years to come).[15]

---

14   Such a gender imbalance, which appears to be quite typical of these discussions, also exemplified the makeup of the geoengineering panel, at the 3rd Annual UC Santa Cruz Climate Science and Policy Conference (February 26–27, 2016), which featured Slawek Tulaczyk, Waleed Abdalati, Jeffrey Kiehl, Michael Kraft, and Alan Robock.

15   The Center for Biological Diversity, reporting in 2011, writes: "We found that the oil spill has likely harmed or killed approximately 82,000 birds of 102 species, approximately 6,165 sea turtles, and up to 25,900 marine mammals, including bottlenose dolphins, spinner dolphins, melon-headed whales and sperm whales. The spill also harmed an unknown number of fish—including bluefin tuna and substantial habitat for our nation's smallest seahorse—and an unknown but likely catastrophic number of crabs, oysters, corals and other sea life." They also point out that the toll will continue to mount in the future. "A Deadly Toll: The Gulf Oil Spill and the Unfolding Wildlife Disaster," *Center for Biological Diversity*, accessed June 9, 2016, http://www.biologicaldiversity.org/programs/public_lands/energy/dirty_energy _development/oil_and_gas/gulf_oil_spill/a_deadly_toll.html.

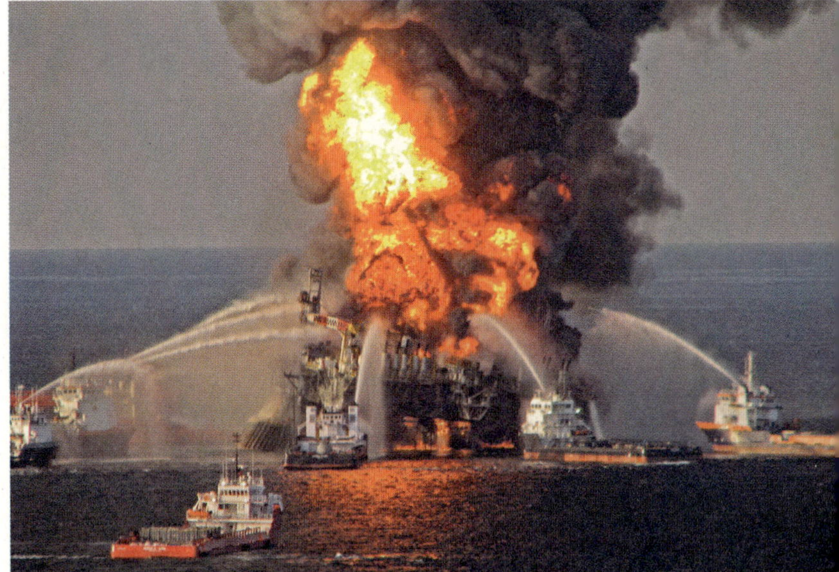

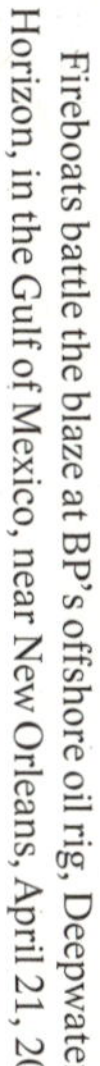

Fireboats battle the blaze at BP's offshore oil rig, Deepwater Horizon, in the Gulf of Mexico, near New Orleans, April 21, 2010

And of course there was the notorious "spillcam," BP's live video feed of the leak, the submarine coverage made public only following congressional pressure on the corporation, resisting exposure at every turn. The nonstop flow of images captured the uninterrupted gushing oil, approximately ninety-five thousand barrels a day, over three months. The webcam in particular made evident the cruel and unbearable impotence of viewers who found themselves, as I remember my own experience, glued to their screens, mastering the image of the horrendous leak but not being able to do anything to stop the flow.

Undoubtedly these images have had a positive impact on public environmental consciousness, at the time critically raising awareness of the ongoing risks of extreme deepwater oil drilling—risks that are subsequently being tested in relation to the desire of Shell and other corporations to drill in the Arctic in harsh, uncontrollable maritime conditions. Yet images of eco-catastrophe have also

Still from BP's underwater "spillcam," Deepwater Horizon, Gulf of Mexico, July 10, 2010

worked toward radically different purposes, granting supporting reassurance to the otherwise false claim that cleanup efforts following industrial accidents have been efficient and effective. This is evidenced in American commercial media conglomerate CBS's report from 2013 on the aftermath of the BP oil spill, accompanied by many of the very same images that initially helped raise the alarm: "Due to the extensive cleanup effort, early restoration projects and natural recovery processes," they happily announced, "much of the Gulf has returned to its baseline condition; the condition it would be in if the accident had not occurred."[16]

Not only is it evident that mainstream media characteristically operates in league with fossil fuel corporations—indeed BP's own

16   Jessica Hartogs, "Three Years after BP Oil Spill, Active Clean-Up Ends in Three States," *CBS News*, June 10, 2013, http://www.cbsnews.com/news/three-years-after-bp-oil-spill-active-clean-up-ends-in-three-states/. On the history of environmental accidents, from the 1969 Union Oil spill in the Santa Barbara channel to the nuclear meltdown at Three Mile Island in 1979 to the 1989 Exxon Valdez Alaskan oil spill, and the tendency of corporations and mainstream media to claim that nature will repair itself, see Dunaway, *Seeing Green*, chap. 1n27.

press release repeats verbatim CBS's report[17]—but CBS's manifestly false claim points to the uneven effects of eco-catastrophe visuality where identical images, when placed in different contexts, can support multiple interpretations with divergent, even opposing, political implications. When the developmentalist, capitalist, and growth-obsessed petro-economy forms the unexamined and assumed economic ground on which conventional politics take place—as when there can be no government-proposed political solution to address climate change that does not begin with reaffirming the so-called free market—then we can only expect the corporate media to direct the circulation and interpretation of these images in ways that suit their interests. When market-based financial flows are used to interpret and determine biochemical ones, in a system run by geocrats, we confront the contemporary approximation of what André Gorz once called "eco-fascism."[18] Perhaps the Anthropocene is now best described as the age of "corporate activities."

In their cogent reading of the BP media-image repertoire, Peter Galison and Caroline Jones usefully call attention to the "invisibilities" that are part of "a system in which the seen is supported and enabled by the unseen."[19] This situation requires a political analysis that addresses the complexity of environmental media visuality. They point to the vast subsurface oil plumes that have formed in the ocean and drifted far from their site of origin, equaling more than 75 percent of the remaining leaked oil (some thirty million gallons) that has mixed with the nearly two million gallons of

---

17 See BP's press release: "The large-scale cleanup effort, combined with early restoration projects and natural recovery processes, is helping the Gulf return to its baseline condition, which is the condition it would be in if the accident had not occurred." "Active Shoreline Cleanup Operations from Deepwater Horizon Accident End," *BP Global*, April 15, 2014, http://www.bp.com/en/global/corporate/press/press-releases/active-shoreline-cleanup-operations-dwh-accident-end.html.

18 André Gorz, *Ecology as Politics*, trans. Patsy Vigderman and Jonathan Cloud (Boston: South End Press, 1980); this reference is also cited in Bonneuil and Fressoz, "Who Is the Anthropos?," 93.

19 Peter Galison and Caroline A. Jones, "Unknown Quantities," *Artforum*, November 2010, 51.

"Corexit" chemical dispersant applied by BP to the water surface to fragment the crude and make it sink. Thus invisible, the dispersed oil goes un-imaged, drifting as well—and most importantly for the corporation—from public imagination. It is true that BP eventually agreed to pay $18.7 billion in a sweeping oil spill settlement in July 2015, seemingly a substantial verdict; yet, as Charlie Tebbutt of the Center for Biological Diversity points out in a *Democracy Now!* report, the sum merely amounts to what the corporation makes in profit every three months, and two thirds of it can be written off as a tax break.[20] Corporate economics is similarly an arena whose visibilities and invisibilities are carefully choreographed, where one set determines the other.

For Galison and Jones, "The circuit—of drill, spill, 'clean up,' and drill again—relies on such systems of images and occlusions, in which the production of invisibility forms an aesthetic chiaroscuro to all the tragic, sublime, and subaquatic flows"; therefore, "Our response must be to take what's out of sight, and keep it well in mind."[21] One can only agree. Meanwhile, the gulf has definitely not returned to its baseline condition. This was clear when writer Antonia Juhasz accompanied a team of scientists as they collected animal, plant, water, and sediment samples from the seabed's fragile ecosystem five years after the spill, providing ample evidence that contests BP's claim that there has been "very limited impact from the oil spill on the seafloor." "If you short-circuit the bottom," Dr. Samantha Joye, a biogeochemist at the University of Georgia, told

20 See "BP to Pay $18.7B in Sweeping Oil Spill Settlement," *Democracy Now!*, July 6, 2015, http://www.democracynow.org/2015/7/6/headlines/bp_to_pay_187b_in_sweeping _oil_spill_settlement; and Nika Knight, "Tax Windfall for BP Makes Deepwater Horizon Settlement a 'Major Coup' for Oil Giant," *Common Dreams*, April 5, 2016, http://commondreams.org/news/2016/04/05/tax-windfall-bp-makes-deepwater -horizon-settlement-major-coup-oil-giant.

21 Galison and Jones, "Unknown Quantities," 51. Also, on the possible eco-politics of the unseen and unseeable, see Julie Doyle, "Picturing the Clima(c)tic: Greenpeace and the Representational Politics of Climate Change Communication," *Science as Culture* 16, no. 2 (June 2007): 129–50.

Juhasz, "you threaten the entire cycle. Without a healthy ocean, we'll all be dead."[22] Where will the Anthropocenologists leave us?

How can we mobilize politically around a catastrophe's invisibilities, given our culture's fixation on the spectacular production of images framed with happy Hollywood endings, leading to the seeming inevitable denouement of CBS's report quoted above: a media fiction, as "if the accident had not occurred"? And how to combat images that work toward assuring us of the controllability of climate change, even while they reinforce the idea that we are all responsible, insofar as we humans are all part of anthropos, and that anthropos can conquer all?

Of course, ultimately, it is not even the industrial accidents that are of greatest concern, even though these events and their effects—oil spills, burning platforms, human death tolls, oil-drenched shores, and massive animal die-offs—are truly catastrophic and depressing. Rather, it is the uninterrupted, accident-free, normal running of the fossil fuel economy, now poised to be super-charged in the US by the Trump administration, that is the ultimate threat and should be the focus of our attention, politically, economically, and ecologically. Mainstream media images, in this regard, often contribute not so much to the responsible use of technology, but to an ideological mechanism of reassurance, framed within debates that appear to give balanced perspective to all sides—but of course they do not. Ultimately, they form part of the very technological apparatus of advanced capitalism that has created the environmental problems in the first place, including a carefully edited selection of visuality that reinforces the premises of the Anthropocene. What would the visuality of a culture against the Anthropocene look like?

---

22   See Antonia Juhasz, "Thirty Million Gallons under the Sea: Following the Trail of BP's Oil in the Gulf of Mexico," *Harper's Magazine*, June 2015, http://harpers.org/archive/2015/06/thirty-million-gallons-under-the-sea/1/. Also see Antonia Juhasz, *Black Tide: The Devastating Impact of the Gulf Oil Spill* (New York: John Wiley and Sons, 2011); and Antonia Juhasz, *The Tyranny of Oil: The World's Most Powerful Industry—And What We Must Do to Stop It* (New York: William Morrow, 2009).

Chapter Three

Against the Anthropocene

On May 16, 2015, the Paddle in Seattle demonstration sHell No! unleashed its kayak flotilla, a mass direct action against Shell's Arctic-bound Polar Pioneer drilling rig temporarily stationed in the West Coast city's port. The rig was on its way to the Chukchi Sea in the Arctic Ocean, under contract from Transocean, the same corporation whose Deepwater Horizon oil rig, drilling for BP, was responsible for the oil spill catastrophe in the Gulf of Mexico five years earlier. Shell hoped to begin oil exploration in the Arctic where the sea ice has begun to subside during the summers owing to global warming. In other words—with no small degree of irony—the corporation intended to take advantage of climate change in order to extract more of the same fossil fuel that caused the melting in the first place.[1] The kayaktivists hoped to block its way, preventing it from leaving port, or to at least delay its departure, and create

---

1   On the corporate and state race to extract oil and natural gas in the Arctic, see Subhankar Banerjee, "In the Warming Arctic Seas," in "Climate's Cliff," special issue, *World Policy Journal* 32, no. 2 (Summer 2015), http://www.worldpolicy.org/journal/summer2015/in-the-warming-arctic-seas.

a media firestorm to help shift public opinion against extreme forms of petrocapitalist extraction.

Word and images of the Paddle in Seattle protest, organized by environmental groups including Rising Tide Seattle, Stop Shell Seattle, Bayan Pacific Northwest, 350 Seattle, Backbone Campaign, and ShellNo Action Council, and joined by Greenpeace and Indigenous activists, spread widely online.[2] They accompanied reports in indie media and mainstream press, adding momentum to the popular challenge to offshore drilling in the far north. In fact, Shell's Arctic exploration was already marked by a history of industrial accident. In late 2012, one of the company's drill barges, the *Kulluk*, had drifted out of control in stormy weather, while on its way to the north, and run aground on Sitkalidak Island in the western Gulf of Alaska, after its tow line broke off from the *Aiviq*, the icebreaking tug.[3] It was therefore surprising that the Obama administration approved the corporation's request three years later to conduct further drilling in the pristine and remote Chukchi Sea, despite grave concern expressed by environmentalists that the fragile area is prone to extreme weather and, with no airports or rail lines nearby, nearly impossible for rescue and cleanup crews to reach in the likely event of disaster. An oil spill in this region would indeed be catastrophic— a glaringly obvious realization that motivated the Paddle in Seattle (so named to honor the infamous anti-World Trade Organization's Battle in Seattle mass demonstration in 1999, which set off the anti-corporate globalization movement that has grown ever since).[4] When Shell opted to postpone its Arctic drilling plans in September 2015, followed the next month by President Obama's reversal of his earlier decision to grant the corporation Arctic oil leases, it was in no

2   See *sHELLNO.org*, accessed September 20, 2016, http://shellnodotorg.tumblr.com/.

3   See McKenzie Funk, "The Wreck of the *Kulluk*," *New York Times Magazine*, December 30, 2014, http://www.nytimes.com/2015/01/04/magazine/the-wreck-of-the-kulluk.html?_r=0.

4   See Rebecca Solnit and David Solnit, *The Battle of the Story of the Battle of Seattle* (Oakland, CA: AK Press, 2009).

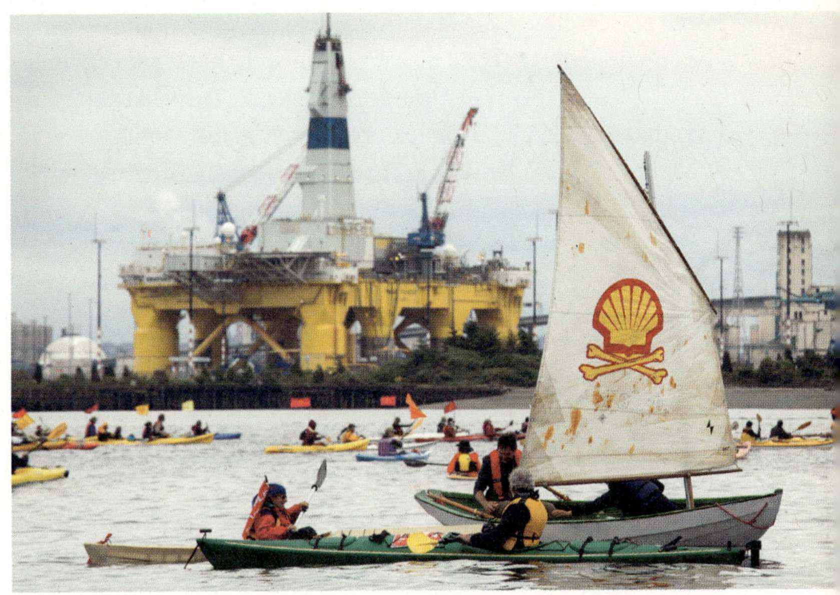

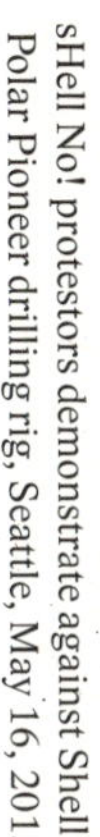

sHell No! protestors demonstrate against Shell's Polar Pioneer drilling rig, Seattle, May 16, 2015

small part owing to the immense pressure from environmentalists and activists, which Shell itself publically acknowledged.[5]

That pressure is visualized in the images of the sHell No! blockade, which have energized the mounting antagonism between corporate industry's pushing of us into climate chaos, and grassroots campaigners' opposition to the continued extraction of fossil fuel. "Our culture and livelihood is dependent on the bowhead, the walrus, the seal and the fish," explained Inupiaq activist Mae Hank, as reported on the website of the First Nations movement Idle No More. He referred to the various sea creatures on which Inupiaq people depend for their food.

---

5   See Arthur Neslen, "Shell Has Frozen Its Arctic Oil Drilling—But It's Still Hungry for Fossil Fuels," *Guardian*, September 28, 2015, https://www.theguardian.com/environment/2015/sep/28/shell-has-frozen-its-arctic-oil-drilling-but-the-fight-isnt-over; and Mark Engler, "#ShellNo: The Triumph of the Kayaktivists," *New Internationalist*, December 21, 2015, http://newint.org/columns/mark-engler/2015/12/01/kayaktivists-victory/.

"How can Shell go ahead with such a risky operation"—with a 75 percent likelihood of a disastrous oil spill that would decimate sea life—"when peoples' lives are at stake?"[6] The kayak blockade surrounded the Polar Pioneer, creating a floating model of what Ana Fiegenbaum, Fabian Frenzel, and Patrick McCurdy call a "biopolitical assemblage," an apt description of a protest camp.[7] As Yates McKee glosses the term in his book on activist art in the post-Occupy condition, such an assemblage is comprised of "living subjects, physical space, material infrastructure, technological devices, cultural forms, and organization practices that simultaneously stage dissent against the status quo while prefiguring 'alternative worlds.'"[8] In this case, the "subjects" represent a heterogeneous and transnational alliance of environmentalists, NGO representatives, and Indigenous activists; the "physical space" designates the normally uncontested maritime transit point between industrial port and offshore extraction site; the "material infrastructure" identifies the creatively deployed kayaks, leisure crafts retooled for rebellious intervention and nonviolent direct action; the "technological devices" point toward the Internet-based activist networks and alternative media distribution platforms that were instrumental in organizing and publicizing the convergence; and the "cultural forms" are a mix of political theater, mediagenic banners and signage, civil disobedience, and Indigenous ritual—all joining

---

6   Quoted in "'Shell No!' Indigenous Activists to Confront Shell to End Arctic Drilling at Shareholder Meetings in Netherlands and London," *Idle No More*, May 18, 2015, http://www .idlenomore.ca/shell_no. Idle No More is an Indigenous resurgence movement in Canada that supports "the peaceful revolution, to honour Indigenous sovereignty, and to protect the land and water." See The Kino-nda-niimi Collective, ed., *The Winter We Danced: Voices from the Past, the Future, and the Idle No More Movement* (Winnipeg: ARP Books, 2014); and on the visual politics of this movement, see India Rael Young, "Momentum: The Ripple of Art Activism from Idle No More," *Hemisphere* 7 (2014): 76–92.

7   Ana Fiegenbaum, Fabian Frenzel, and Patrick McCurdy, *Protest Camps* (London: Zed, 2013).

8   Yates McKee, *Strike Art: Contemporary Art and the Post-Occupy Condition* (London: Verso, 2016), 101.

together to create a stage of joyful dissent, a mobilization for future survival, and a prefiguration of a post-fossil fuel world where corporations (if they exist at all) are held accountable for their operations.

The action came amid a wave of similar blockades posed against fossil fuel extraction points and energy pipelines that carry crude hundreds of miles through fragile ecosystems, agricultural lands, aquifers, and waterways, and inhabited areas to distant refineries and transportation hubs. As such, the sHell No! protest is part of what activists and Naomi Klein calls "blockadia," the grass-roots climate activism composed of encampments and occupations, many in Indigenous territories, many made up of transnational alliances (as with the effort against the $7 billion Keystone XL pipeline project), that is sweeping the globe, intent on shutting down the infrastructure of petrocapitalism at a time of climate emergency.[9] Notable examples include the Unist'ot'en Camp, stationed within the Wet'suwet'en First Nation, currently blocking five major pipeline proposals (including Coast GasLink, Enbridge Northern Gateway, and Pacific Trails pipeline projects) that hope to carry crude to Prince Rupert and Kitimat refineries from the Albertan tar sands and additional extraction points in British Columbia, a conflict couched within longstanding First Nations territory disputes and treaty conflicts that have formed part of the history of Canadian settler colonialism.[10] There is also the current protest camp called Sacred Stone, assembled by members of the Standing Rock Sioux tribe, in North Dakota. There, hundreds of Indigenous nations and allied environmental activists have shut down construction on the multibillion-dollar Dakota Access pipeline, intended to carry Bakken crude from North Dakota to Illinois, threatening the water supplies of millions along the 1,134-mile-long (1,825 km) route

---

9   See Naomi Klein, "Blockadia: The New Climate Warriors," in *This Changes Everything*, 293–337.

10   See *Unist'ot'en Camp*, accessed September 20, 2016, http://unistoten.camp/.

(though one of Trump's first executive orders upon taking office in early 2017 is to revitalize the pipeline project).[11] More abstractly, but relevant to our analysis, the sHell No! action throws a wedge into the universalizing logic of the Anthropocene, a term that, as we have seen, suggests—falsely—that we are all agents of climate change, sharing equally in its causes and effects.

More specifically, Hank's sHell No! statement, along with the kayak action and other scenes from contemporary blockadia, together put the lie to the "Ecomodernist Manifesto" that makes the case that "we" must seize the opportunity to create (read: geoengineer) a "good Anthropocene," "decoupling" economic growth from environmental impacts. Bringing together eco-optimist luminaries like Stewart Brand, Erle Ellis, Ted Nordhaus, and Michael Shellenberger, the group argues that, despite environmental setbacks, "humans" must continue down the path of modernization, using "their growing social, economic, and technological powers to make life better for people, stabilize the climate, and protect the natural world."[12] It is not surprising that among this group is techno-utopian Mark Lynas, author of *The God Species: Saving the Planet in the Age of Humans* (2011), whose neo-Prometheanism takes literally comember Brand's *Whole Earth Catalog* motto of the late 1960s: "We are as gods and might as well get good at it," which Brand himself has developed in recent publications such as *Whole Earth Discipline: Why Dense Cities, Nuclear Power, Transgenic Crops, Restored Wildlands, and Geoengineering Are Necessary*.[13] A certain deification of anthropos

---

11   See "Stopping the Snake: Indigenous Protesters Shut Down Construction of Dakota Access Pipeline," *Democracy Now!*, August 18, 2016, http://www.democracynow.org/2016/8/18 /stopping_the_snake_indigenous_protesters_shut.

12   John Asafu-Adjaye et al., "An Ecomodernist Manifesto," April 2015, http://www.ecomodern ism.org/s/An-Ecomodernist-Manifesto.pdf, 6.

13   Stewart Brand, *Whole Earth Discipline: Why Dense Cities, Nuclear Power, Transgenic Crops, Restored Wildlands, and Geoengineering Are Necessary* (New York: Penguin, 2009). For a critical study of Brand's publication, see Fred Turner, *From Counterculture to*

is in evidence here, with a startling hubris that goes much further than the ancients ever did. Indeed, as South African anthropologist Lesley Green has observed, mockingly: "In the Anthropocene, it is the gods and goddesses of reason in the technosphere who will yield the geocycles to come, and they alone will determine who and what is relinked or delinked among the earth's spheres."[14]

The "Ecomodernist Manifesto," however, is really nothing more than a bad utopian fantasy, based on a form of magical thinking that renews misguided industry-friendly efforts to overcome an earlier "limits to growth" environmentalism, first articulated in the early 1970s.[15] Sickly sweet with optimism, the manifesto is basically an apology for nuclear energy that allows its authors to reassert the imperative of economic development, as if such a capitalist-growth-driven energy system will have no negative impact on earth systems (counter to recent experience in Fukushima). In a comprehensive rebuttal of the Ecomodernist project, the group of writers including the environmental historian Jeremy Caradonna points out:

> Ecomodernism violates everything we know about ecosystems, energy, population, and natural resources. Fatally, it ignores the lessons of ecology and thermodynamics, which teach us

Cyberculture: Stewart Brand, the Whole Earth Network, and the Rise of Digital Utopianism (Chicago: University of Chicago Press, 2006).

14 Lesley Green, "The Changing of the Gods of Reason: Cecil John Rhodes, Karoo Fracking, and the Decolonizing of the Anthropocene," *e-flux journal* 65 (June 9, 2015), http://supercommunity.e-flux.com/texts/the-changing-of-the-gods-of-reason/. She continues: "Whether the incoming gods and goddesses of reason can transform the relations that have made the Anthropocene—where reciprocities and gifts have been replaced by commodities set in a relation of violence—depends on the decolonization of knowledge itself."

15 "Limits to growth" refers to the important 1972 study, commissioned by the Club of Rome, of the relation between exponential socioeconomic growth and finite resources, which predicted catastrophic results if limits to growth were not taken seriously. See Donella H. Meadows et al., *The Limits to Growth: A Report for the Club of Rome's Project on the Predicament of Mankind* (New York: Universe Books, 1972). See also Graham Turner and Cathy Alexander, "Limits to Growth Was Right: New Research Shows We're Nearing Collapse," *Guardian*, September 1, 2014, https://www.theguardian.com/commentisfree/2014/sep/02/limits-to-growth-was-right-new-research-shows-were-nearing-collapse.

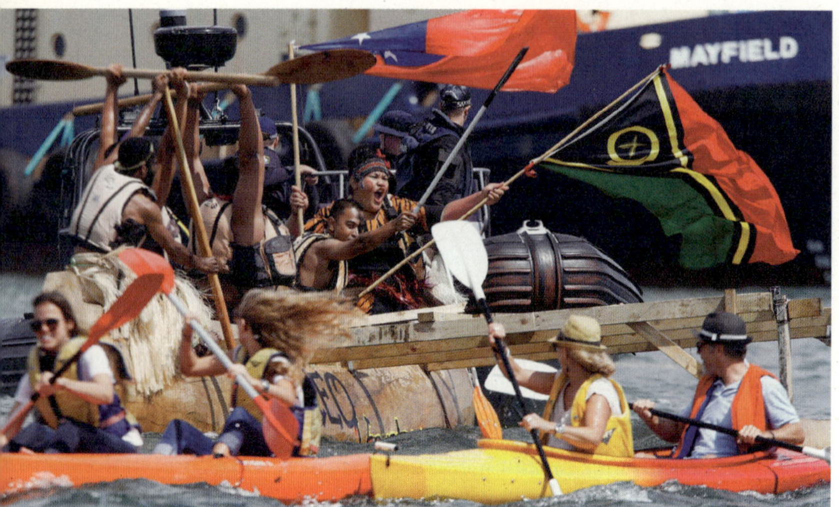

The Pacific Climate Warriors, activists from the Pacific Islands, form a flotilla to blockade the entrance to the world's largest coal port, Newcastle, Australia, October 17, 2014

that species (and societies) have natural limits to growth. The ecomodernists, by contrast, brazenly claim that the limits to growth are a myth, and that human population and the economy could continue to grow almost indefinitely. Moreover, the ecomodernists ignore or downplay many of the ecological ramifications of growth. The *Manifesto* has nothing to say about the impacts of conventional farming, monoculture, pesticide-resistant insects, GMOs, and the increasing privatization of seeds and genetic material. It is silent on the decline of global fisheries or the accumulation of microplastic pollution in the oceans, reductions in biodiversity, threats to ecosystem services, and the extinction of species. Nor does it really question our reliance on fossil fuels. It does argue that societies need to "decarbonize," but the *Manifesto* also tacitly supports coal, oil, and natural gas by advocating for carbon capture and storage.[16]

16 Jeremy Caradonna et al., "A Degrowth Response to an Ecomodernist Manifesto," *Resilience.org*, May 6, 2015, http://www.resilience.org/stories/2015-05-06/a-degrowth -response-to-an-ecomodernist-manifesto.

What is additionally striking about the Ecomodernist document, beyond its factual weaknesses and ecological falsehoods, is that there is no mention of social justice or democratic politics, no mention of social movements or justice "from below," no acknowledgement of the fact that big technologies like nuclear reinforce centralized power, the military-industrial complex, and the inequalities of corporate globalization, rather than the distributed self-sufficient economies and egalitarian local governance that typically accompanies renewable energy paradigms (as exemplified, on a micro scale, by the human-powered kayaktivists).

This is not an anomaly. The Anthropocene thesis tends to support such developmentalist globalization, joining all humans together in shared responsibility for creating our present environmental disaster. Exploiting further its universalizing logic, the Anthropocene concept makes it easy to justify further technological interventions in the earth's systems via geoengineering, as if the causes of climate disruption can be its solutions. In such narratives as these, anthropos serves to distract attention from the economic class that has long benefitted from the financial system responsible for catastrophic environmental change. As noted by Heather Davis and Etienne Turpin in their insightful introduction to *Art in the Anthropocene*, "the Anthropocene is not simply the result of activities undertaken by the species *Homo sapiens*; instead, these effects derive from a *particular* nexus of epistemic, technological, social, and political economic coalescences figured in the contemporary reality of petrocapitalism."[17] If so, then at least we can refer to it as the "petrocapitalist Anthropocene": that is, an epoch when "nature is made visible only as 'natural capital' in economic trade-offs, or as a backdrop to a techno-optimism that places our

---

17   Heather Davis and Etienne Turpin, "Art & Death: Lives between the Fifth Assessment & the Sixth Extinction," in *Art in the Anthropocene: Encounters among Aesthetics, Politics, Environments and Epistemologies*, ed. Heather Davis and Etienne Turpin (London: Open Humanities Press, 2015), 7.

collective fate in the hands of markets and technology," as Katrina Forrester observes.[18]

Even Bruno Latour, otherwise given over to adopting Anthropocene vocabulary (and liberally using its universalizing rhetoric of "human agency"),[19] recognizes its propensity to disavow the differential responsibilities of climate change: "Hundreds of different people"—such as Indigenous nations in the Amazonian forest, the impoverished in the slums of Mumbai, and workers subjected to long commutes owing to lack of affordable housing—"will at once raise their voice and say they feel no responsibility whatsoever for those deeds at a geological scale."[20] That is, even as he validates the concept of the Anthropocene so long as *anthropos* signifies— against its very terminological implications—a differentiated "people with contradictory interest, opposing cosmoses," and "warring entities."[21]

The case is similar with Dipesh Chakrabarty, another leading light of humanities-based Anthropocene theorization, who writes that "a critique of capital is not sufficient for addressing questions relating to human history once the crisis of climate change has been acknowledged and the Anthropocene has begun to loom on the horizon of our present. The geologic now of the Anthropocene has become entangled with the now of *human history*."[22] What is strik-

---

18 Katrina Forrester, "The Anthropocene Truism," *Nation*, May 12, 2016, https://www.the nation.com/article/the-anthropocene-truism/.

19 See, for instance, Bruno Latour, "Agency at the Time of the Anthropocene," *New Literary History* 45, no. 1 (Winter 2014): 1–18.

20 Bruno Latour, "The Anthropocene and the Destruction of the Image of the Globe" (lecture, "Facing Gaia: Six Lectures on the Political Theology of Nature," Gifford Lectures on Natural Religion, University of Edinburgh, February 18–28, 2013), available here: http://macaulay.cuny.edu/eportfolios/wakefield15/files/2015/01/LATOUR-GIFFORD -SIX-LECTURES_1.pdf, 80. Of course Paul Crutzen and other Anthropocene proponents likely realize that a minority of humanity have actually been historically responsible for current geological changes. My point is to investigate what thoughts and practices the term nonetheless ends up licensing.

21 Ibid., 81.

22 Dipesh Chakrabarty, "The Climate of History: Four Theses," *Critical Inquiry* 35 (Winter 2009): 212 (my emphasis).

ing here is Chakrabarty's disavowing of the framework of inequality and difference otherwise foregrounded in his earlier practice of an economically and politically attuned method of analysis. As Christophe Bonneuil and Jean-Baptiste Fressoz observe in their own critical discussion of the Anthropocene thesis, "[Chakrabarty's] manner of envisaging causalities by placing humanity in the narrative as a universal agent, indifferently responsible, illustrates the abandoning of the grid of Marxist and postcolonial reading in favour of an undifferentiated humanity."[23]

Despite the critical interrogations of the Anthropocene by diverse commentators (such as Davis and Turpin, who in the end nonetheless implicitly endorse the term even as they importantly qualify its usage), we might challenge the viability of this conceptualization altogether. And the growth of inspiring visual culture, tied in to social movements, posed *against* the Anthropocene is one reason why. The expanding photographic record makes clear that there exists significant rejection of the term's conceptual bases in today's social movements and their visual cultures, particularly given the numerous images embedded in independent media that depict the destructiveness of the industrial economy and its catastrophic impact on diverse "human" communities, including Indigenous peoples and rural working classes, as well as on the (ever-shrinking) biodiverse web of life beyond the human.

---

23 Bonneuil and Fressoz, "Who Is the Anthropos?," 67. Of course there are also eco-Marxists who support the "A" term as well, who warn that the Left risks walling off science when it criticizes and discounts its depoliticized research. See, for example, Ian Angus, "Entering the Age of Humans," *Socialist Review* (May 2016), http://socialistreview.org.uk/413/entering-age-humans, who writes: "If we condemn it from the sidelines, we will be leaving Anthropocene science and scientists under the ideological sway of neoliberalism, and we will be irrelevant to the most important scientific development of our time." I am in agreement that we must indeed "seize this remarkable opportunity to unite the latest scientific findings with an ecological Marxist analysis in a socio-ecological account of the origins, nature and direction of the crisis." Yet that does not mean simply accepting scientists' terminological proposals and their implications without critical examination or radical alternative.

One powerful example of Anthropocene resistance is the rebellion that has taken place around the Albertan tar sands and the related Keystone XL oil pipeline that industry hopes will link Canadian extraction to Houston's refineries—even after the Obama administration at last rejected the proposed completion of the project in November 2015, after more than six years of review and considerable environmental activism. The southern portion is built, and if the rest is completed (as Trump's extractivist regime desires), it would cross nearly two thousand American waterways, including the Ogallala Aquifer, source of one-third of the country's farmland irrigation, and, according to climate scientist James Hansen, would mean "game over for the climate" owing to the greenhouse gas emissions that would result from burning through its oil.[24] This extraction project is significant not only because it represents a massive befouling of the environment—the largest of its kind on Earth—but also because this is not a case of industrial accident or oil spill, as was Exxon Valdez in 1989 or BP's Deepwater Horizon in 2006 (both of which Shell and other corporations intend to risk in the future), even though that is an ongoing danger of such a transportation system. Nor is it yet another instance of the corporate media's many spectacles of postapocalyptic futures reveling in what the Breakthrough Institute terms the "bad" Anthropocene, as in the drought-ravaged, violence-obsessed, and resource-scarce narratives of films like *Mad Max: Fury Road* (2015), representing one scenario of things to come, which works ideologically to encourage blind faith in the "good" Anthropocene.[25] Rather than

---

24 James Hansen, "Game Over for the Climate," *New York Times*, May 9, 2012, http://www .nytimes.com/2012/05/10/opinion/game-over-for-the-climate.html?_r=0.

25 Amelia Urry, Suzanne Jacobs, and Ted Alvarez, "Mad Max: Fury Road May Be the Anthropocene at Its Worst—But It Makes for Pretty Sick Cinema," *Grist*, May 15, 2015, http://grist.org/living/mad-max-fury-road-may-be-the-anthropocene-at-its-worst-but -it-makes-for-pretty-sick-cinema/. On the (mis)use value of dystopian futurism, see China Miéville, "The Limits of Utopia," *Salvage*, accessed June 9, 2016, http://

focusing on failures of industry and dystopian futurist visions, which serve only to divert us from the real problem at hand, tar sands development is shocking because it concerns the normal, accident-free running of petrocapitalism that is itself bringing disastrous effects on us—with some affected more than others—in the present.[26]

As Eriel Tchekwie Deranger, activist and spokesperson for the Athabasca Chipewyan First Nation, explains, tar sands oil extraction represents a mode of strip-mining that produces a viscous, dirty crude, or diluted bitumen, and, with an affected area equivalent to the size of England, its industrial zone is considered the most ecologically destructive project currently on the planet.[27] The synthetic slurry of tar sands oil, solid in its natural state, must be processed into flowing liquid for transportation by being boiled and diluted with toxic chemicals and gas condensates, using copious amounts of water. The reason corporations are turning to such dirty oil sources entailing extreme extraction technology is that easier-to-reach liquid crude has been fully tapped: tar sands oil, offshore deep water drilling, hydraulic fracturing (fracking), and horizontal drilling are what remain as current options in our fossil-fuel obsessed present, heading us on a course of environmental suicide. Indeed, the industrial

salvage.zone/mieville_all.html; and Margaret Atwood, "It's Not Climate Change, It's Everything Change," *Medium*, July 27, 2015, https://medium.com/matter/it-s-not -climate-change-it-s-everything-change-8fd9aa671804.

26 Here I am in agreement with Donna Haraway: true engagement today—what Haraway calls "staying with the trouble"—"requires learning to be truly present, not as a vanishing pivot between awful or edenic pasts and apocalyptic or salvific futures, but as mortal critters entwined in myriad unfinished configurations of places, times, matters, meanings." Donna J. Haraway, *Staying with the Trouble: Making Kin in the Chthulucene* (Durham, NC: Duke University Press, 2016), 1.

27 See Eriel Tchekwie Deranger, presentation, "Rights of Nature," conference, Nottingham Contemporary, January 24, 2015, http://www.nottinghamcontemporary.org/event/rights -nature-conference. See also Gaia Foundation, "Canada, Alberta Tar Sands—the Most Destructive Project on Earth," accessed June 9, 2016, http://www.gaiafoundation.org /canada-alberta-tar-sands-the-most-destructive-project-on-earth (page discontinued).

ecocide has rendered Fort Chipewyan, home to Deranger's people living in the Athabasca river region and its boreal forests, a toxic wasteland. This destruction is shown in photographs like David Dodge's anti-spectacular image of Alberta tar sands development (which serves to illustrate Deranger's comments presented in a recent *Nation* article),[28] depicting the region as a massive wound of industrial mining. Composed of concentric rings of toxic tailing ponds filled with the copious amounts of wastewater needed to process bitumen, the lifeless black grey surface, devoid of its thousands-of-years-old boreal forests (derided as "overburden" by extraction companies), is visible only through miasmic clouds of polluting fumes. In addition, numerous documentary films— such as *Kahsatstenhsera: Indigenous Resistance to Tar Sands Pipelines* (2013), produced by Amanda Lickers, Reclaim Turtle Island, and subMedia.tv; *Blockadia Rising: Voices from the Tar Sands Blockade* (2013), directed by Garrett Graham; and Warren Cariou and Neil McArthur's *Land of Oil and Water: Indigenous Voices in Canada's Oil Sands* (2009)—portray the situation of First Nations people on the ground, living and dying in the vicinity of the extraction, as well as their protest singing and dancing, blockades, and direct actions. As the short video *Kahsatstenhsera*, meaning "strength in unity" in Mohawk, explains: "Resistance to all forms of resource extraction and their infrastructure— pipelines, pumping stations, seismic trucks, marine terminals, gas wells and their corporate headquarters—is necessary. As Indigenous peoples, we have a responsibility to our Mother Earth, to the faces not yet born, and all members of creation, to insure that the death machine of colonial capitalism is abolished." The situation of environmental injustice is similar elsewhere: like the Athabasca Chipewyan, minority and low-income communities

---

28   See Wen Stephenson, "Keystone XL and Tar Sands: Voices from the Front Lines," *Nation* (blog), February 4, 2014, http://www.thenation.com/blog/178224/keystone-xl-and -tar-sands-voices-front-lines.

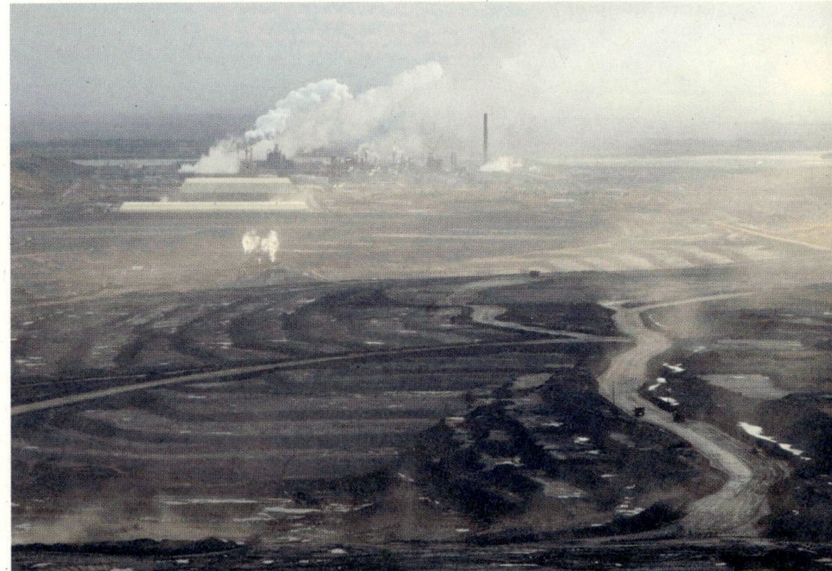

David Dodge, Syncrude oil-sands mining operations with upgrader plant in the background, Alberta, Canada, 2007

living on the edges of the massive petrochemical infrastructure in Houston suffer greatly elevated risks of contracting leukemia and cancers owing to exposure to oil industry pollution.[29]

The Anthropocene simply fails to capture the divisions and antagonism at play here. Yet the resistance is mounting, as Deranger's example of protest suggests. Zoe Todd (Red River Métis/Otipemisiwak), for instance, argues for the need to "Indigenize the Anthropocene"—meaning, for Todd, that "the academy must dismantle the underlying heteropatriarchal and white supremacist structures that shape its current configurations and conversations," including that of the Anthropocene, and commit to what Brazilian

29 As Juan Parras, founder of the group Texas Environmental Justice Advocacy Services, explains in Cherri Foytlin, "Houston Residents Worry about Burden of Keystone XL Pipeline on Local Neighborhood," *Bridge the Gulf* (blog), November 29, 2012, http://bridgethegulf project.org/blog/2012/houston-residents-worry-about-burden-keystone-xl-pipeline-local -neighborhood; and Gaia Foundation, "Canada, Alberta Tar Sands."

anthropologist Eduardo Viveiros de Castro terms "the permanent exercise in the decolonization of thought."[30] In this case, one fundamental element of that decolonization is to challenge the very viability of the petrocapitalist economy, connecting its exploitation of the environment to its exploitation of the disenfranchised, impoverished, and brutalized segments of the population, and opposing its interlinked system, which signals the intersectional basis of an activist political ecology today.[31]

Yet perhaps this move ultimately entails opposing the Anthropocene's very phraseology. As Klein observes, the Anthropocene thesis carries an "unspoken meaning: that humans are a single type, that human nature can be essentialized to the traits that created this crisis" and that, as a result of this choice, "the systems that certain humans created, and other humans powerfully resisted, are completely off the hook. Capitalism, colonialism, patriarchy—those sorts of systems."[32] If so, then it is time to defy the Anthropocene, and no less its conceptualization and practice. Instead, if we are looking for a more accurate and politically enabling geological descriptor, we might consider adopting a term like the "Capitalocene," which appears more precise and exacting. Taken up variously by Andreas Malm, Jason Moore, Donna Haraway, and others in recent years, "Capitalocene" refers to the geological epoch created by corporate globalization, and has the advantage of naming the culprit behind climate change, thereby gathering political traction around itself.[33] The Capitalocene helps

---

30   Zoe Todd, "Indigenizing the Anthropocene," in David and Turpin, *Art in the Anthropocene*, 246, 251; and Eduardo Viveiros de Castro, *Cannibal Metaphysics: For a Post-structural Anthropology*, ed. and trans. Peter Skafish (Minneapolis: Univocal, 2014), 48.

31   For more on intersectionalist ecology, see Demos, *Decolonizing Nature*, 25.

32   Naomi Klein, "Let Them Drown: The Violence of Othering in a Warming World," *London Review of Books*, June 2, 2016, http://www.lrb.co.uk/v38/n11/naomi-klein/let-them-drown.

33   Donna Haraway credits Andreas Malm and Jason W. Moore with the earliest usages of "Capitalocene," in Donna Haraway, "Anthropocene, Capitalocene, Plantationocene, Chthulucene: Making Kin," *Environmental Humanities* 6, no. 1 (2015): 161. Alf Hornborg points out that the "Capitalocene" was coined by Malm at a seminar in Lund in 2009; see Alf

identify the *economic* determination of our geological present. For instance, total oil and gas lobby spending in 2015 in the United States was an astounding $129,876,004, according to the Center for Responsive Politics, which breaks down into the figure of $355,825 *per day*, a financial driver that makes sure that renewable energy is kept off the table and safely away from consumers.[34] In other words, it is not humanity at large that is determining our direction, but rather petrocapitalism's economy in the form of lobbying, greenwashing, climate-change denial, media spectacle, and obfuscation. Similarly, it is not Indigenous peoples, or impoverished communities, or the inhabitants of underdeveloped countries who are subsidizing fossil fuel companies to a degree of $10 million per minute ($5.3 trillion a year) worldwide, so that they can run their Capitalocene enterprises, driving us all toward climate catastrophe, but rather the governments of over-developed nations, as reported recently by the IMF.[35] Klein, in *This Changes Everything*, explains our current global inertia over climate change as follows: "We are stuck because the actions that would give us the best chance of averting catastrophe—and would benefit the vast majority—are extremely threatening to an elite minority that has a stranglehold over our economy, our political process, and most of our major media outlets."[36] It is not that most of us are faultless— many of us drive cars and live in energy-consuming homes, fly to distant places, and use resource-dependent media. Yet low-level

---

Hornborg, "The Political Ecology of the Technocene," in *The Anthropocene and the Global Environmental Crisis: Rethinking Modernity in a New Epoch*, ed. Clive Hamilton, François Gemenne, and Christophe Bonneuil (Abingdon: Routledge, 2015), 67n4. See also: Jason W. Moore, ed., *Anthropocene or Capitalocene: Nature, History, and the Crisis of Capitalism* (Oakland: PM Press, 2016).

34   Figures cited in *Center for Responsive Politics*, accessed September 20, 2016, https://www.opensecrets.org/lobby/top.php?showYear=2015&indexType=i.

35   Nadia Prupis, "Governments Giving Fossil Fuel Companies $10 Million a Minute: IMF," *Common Dreams*, May 18, 2015, http://www.commondreams.org/news/2015/05/18/governments-giving-fossil-fuel-companies-10-million-minute-imf.

36   Klein, *This Changes Everything*, 18.

consumerist complicity is different from structural responsibility. It is the agents of the Capitalocene—corporate and financial elites, petrochemical industry leaders, growth-obsessed pundits—who are doing everything possible, including using their tremendous financial and media resources, to manipulate governments through corporate lobbying, remove sustainable energy options from even entering the discussion, fund climate change deniers, and advocate for continued large-scale and extreme fossil fuel extraction. "Ours is the geological epoch not of humanity, but of capital," as Andreas Malm cogently argues regarding "the Anthropocene myth."[37]

In this regard, contemporary visual culture at its best can play a critical role in raising awareness of the impact, showing the environmental abuse and human costs, of fossil fuel's everyday operations, mediating and encouraging a rebellious activist culture, like the sHell No! protest seen recently in Seattle's port. Such images, the kind circulating in alternative media networks and around which diverse communities and transnational organizations are building political alliances, are working to stop extraction projects, and swaying publics away from the mass media's conventional, depoliticized perspective. Such visual culture—whether documentary photography, indie-media photos, or artistic projects, more on which below—invites us to participate in what Isabelle Stengers terms the "cosmopolitical present," alluding to the progressive composition of a common world, where commonality is predicated upon thinking "in the presence of" those most negatively affected by governmental policies.[38] As

37 Andreas Malm, "The Anthropocene Myth," *Jacobin*, March 30, 2015, https://www.jacobin mag.com/2015/03/anthropocene-capitalism-climate-change/. Additionally there is Erik Swyngedouw's term "Oliganthropocene," "an epoch of a few men and even fewer women." Erik Swyngedouw, "Anthropocenic Promises: The End of Nature, Climate Change and the Process of Post-politicization," accessed September 17, 2016, http://www.bristol.ac.uk/cabot/media/presentations/anthropocene/erikswyngedouw.pdf. We might also propose: "Corporatocene," an epoch ruled by corporations.
38 Isabelle Stengers, "The Cosmopolitical Proposal," in *Making Things Public: Atmospheres of Democracy*, ed. Bruno Latour and Peter Weibel (Cambridge, MA: MIT Press, 2005), 997.

such, contemporary cosmopolitics necessitates thinking critically about the Anthropocene thesis in the company of "those who are so impacted by out-of-control, psychotic, bottom-of-the-barrel resource development, not just here in Canada, but globally," as Deranger insists. "Indigenous people have become the canary in the coal mine. I don't want my children to have to be the sacrifices for humanity to wake up."[39] Photography can help to show why.

---

39   Eriel Tchekwie Deranger, quoted in Stephenson, "Keystone XL and Tar Sands."

Chapter Four

Capitalocene Violence

"Climate change is global-scale violence against places and species, as well as against human beings," writes Rebecca Solnit. "Once we call it by name, we can start having a real conversation about our priorities and values. Because the revolt against brutality begins with a revolt against the language that hides that brutality."[1] Names matter. What we call things matters. In the same vein, Naomi Klein writes: "The grossly unequal distribution of climate impacts"—hurricanes, flooding, forest fires, drought, etc.—"is not some little-understood consequence of the failure to control carbon emissions. It is the result of a series of policy decisions the governments of wealthy countries have made—and continue to make—with full knowledge of the facts and in the face of strenuous objections."[2] Those decisions, informed by a language that hides things, place lives at risk, and not just any lives, but particularly the lives of the

---

1   Rebecca Solnit, "Climate Change Is Violence," *Truthout*, February 5, 2015, http://truth-out.org/progressivepicks/item/28933-climate-change-is-violence.
2   Naomi Klein, "Why #BlackLivesMatter Should Transform the Climate Debate," *Nation*, December 12, 2014, http://www.thenation.com/article/what-does-blacklivesmatter-have-do-climate-change/.

vulnerable, the lives of the impoverished, women, Indigenous peoples, migrants, and people of color. Naming can call attention to these invisibilities. Indeed, "Racism is what has made it possible to systematically look away from the climate threat for more than two decades. It is also what has allowed the worst health impacts of digging up, processing and burning fossil fuels—from cancer clusters to asthma—to be systematically dumped on indigenous communities and on the neighborhoods where people of colour live, work and play."[3] One way to "call violence by name" is to opt for the Capitalocene—the geological age of capitalism—as the term of choice, rather than the misdirected and obfuscating Anthropocene. The terminological distinction invites further critical analysis of Anthropocene conceptualization and visualization, especially in regard to popular media and its image making.

Take *National Geographic*, and science journalist Elizabeth Kolbert's 2011 essay "Enter the Anthropocene—Age of Man," which accepts and thereby provides one more legitimation of the Anthropocene thesis in its opening lines: "It's a new name for a new geologic epoch—one defined by our own massive impact on the planet."[4] Kolbert's text accompanies a photo gallery with images by Edward Burtynsky, the Canadian photographer whose large-scale prints of industrial landscapes are as seductive as they are horrific, as revealing as they are aestheticizing—and aestheticizing in an extremely disturbing manner when it comes to Anthropocene visualizations.

Consider Burtynsky's *Oil Fields #19ab, Belridge, California, USA* (2003), a diptych that shows the San Joaquin Valley's desert petroscape overtaken by an expansive network of pumpjack oil rigs. Captured from a low aerial perspective with an elevated horizon line, the exploited terrain appears patterned by extraction machinery, extending nearly as far as the eye can see. "Discovered in 1911,

---

3   Ibid.
4   Elizabeth Kolbert, "Enter the Anthropocene—Age of Man," *National Geographic*, March 2011, http://ngm.nationalgeographic.com/2011/03/age-of-man/kolbert-text.

this field pumped on as cities were rebuilt for cars and as ancient petroleum molecules were spun into household products such as plastics, cosmetics, and pharmaceuticals," *National Geographic*'s caption explains. "South Belridge today produces 32 million barrels a year—enough for nine hours of world demand." That is, even as Southern California is ever threatened by ongoing climate change violence, including heat waves, a multiyear drought, and catastrophic forest fires.

The photographer's explanation of these images, found on his website, opts for the sanguine: "When I first started photographing industry it was out of a sense of awe at what we as a species were up to. Our achievements became a source of infinite possibilities."[5] Such is typical of Burtynsky's tendency to make monumental, awe-inspiring photographs from scenes of environmental violence—violence defined not only locally in terms of the damage to regional landscapes, but also globally in relation to the contribution of industrial fossil fuel production to climate change. At the same time, those scenes are interpreted as depicting the origins of modern development and the guarantee of the American way of life.

It is true that Burtynsky goes on to signal his own concern with such images, adding the following: "But time goes on, and that flush of wonder began to turn. The car that I drove cross-country began to represent not only freedom, but also something much more conflicted. I began to think about oil itself: as both the source of energy that makes everything possible, and as a source of dread, for its ongoing endangerment of our habitat."[6] Indeed. Yet his images are less about staging that ambivalence—between consumer complicity and industry-led development—and more about dramatizing in spectacular fashion the perverse visual beauty of a technological, and even geological, act of mastery devoid of

---

5   Edward Burtynsky, "OIL—Artist's Statement," accessed June 9, 2016, http://www.edward burtynsky.com/site_contents/Photographs/Oil.html.

6   Ibid.

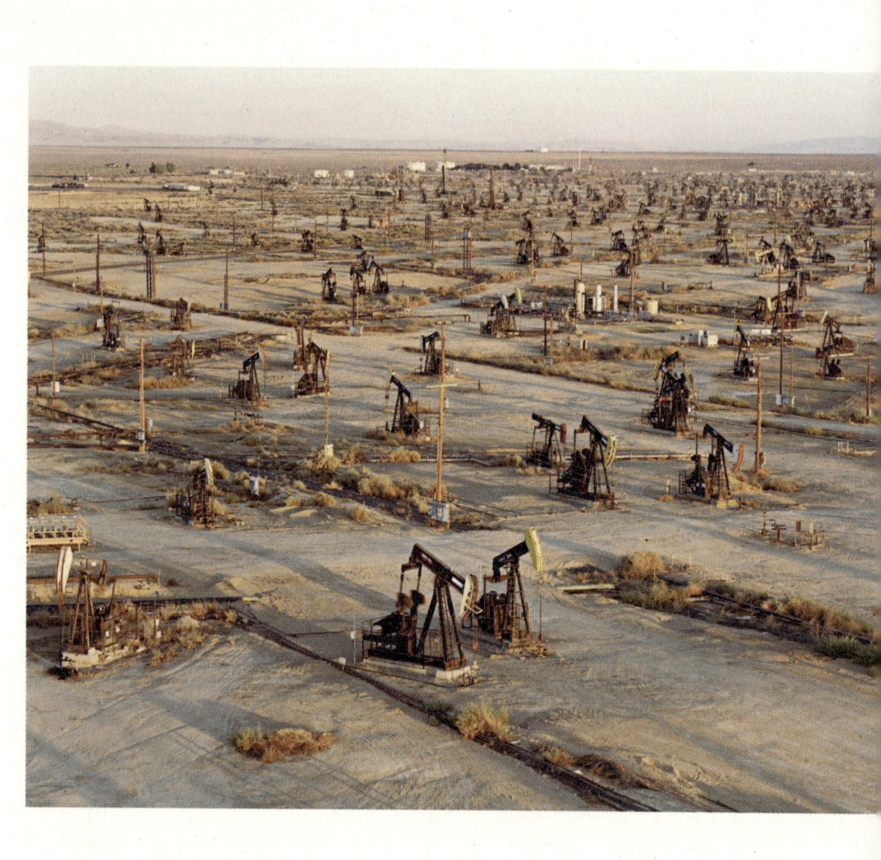

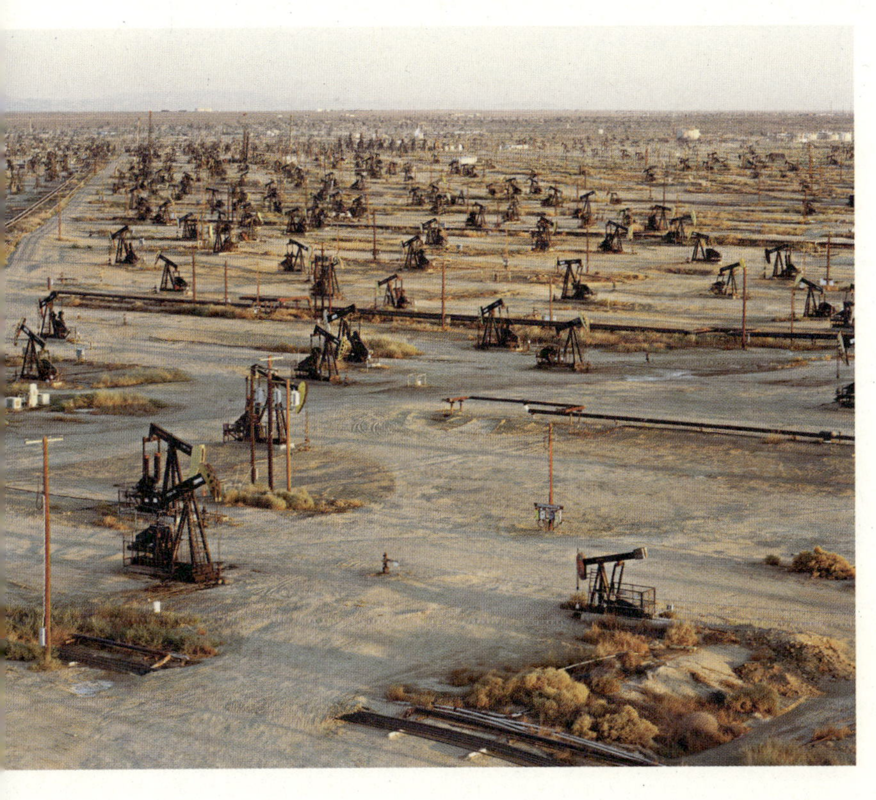

Edward Burtynsky, *Oil Fields #19ab, Belridge, California, USA*, 2003

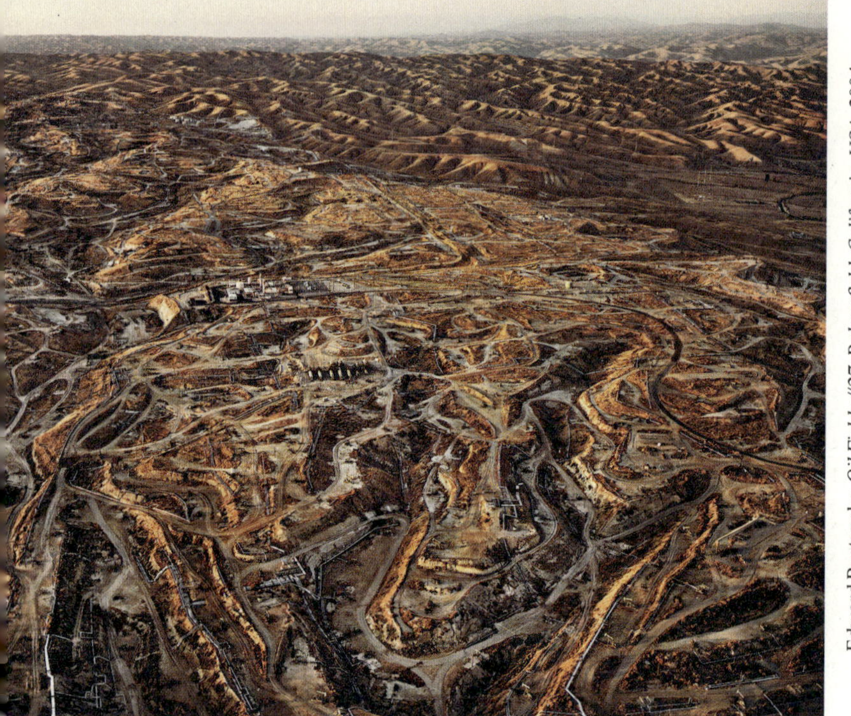

environmental ethics. While Burtynsky is right to point out the con-
sumer-based participation in the oil economy, that frequently made
observation is also part of the ruse that universalizes responsibility
for climate disruption, diverting attention from the fact of corporate
petrocapitalism's enormous economic influence on global politics
that keeps us all locked in its clutches.

Consider also Burtynsky's *Oil Fields #27, Bakersfield, California,
USA* (2004), which depicts a hydrocarbon geography, not far from
Belridge, where the oil infrastructure appears woven into a gold-
bathed chiaroscuro that dramatically patterns this hilly topography.
Here too technology merges with nature, unified aesthetically, com-
posing a picture that is, monstrously, not only visually pleasurable,

but also ostensibly ethically just; an image of American "freedom" whose historical progression, according to the familiar patriotic narrative, is necessary, inevitable, even—as pictured here—beautiful.

What the photographer constructs is the petro-industrial sublime, emphasizing the awesome visuality of the catastrophic oil economy's infrastructure founded on obsessive capitalist growth, which "we as a species," as Burtynsky says, have created. The problem is that such images tend to naturalize petrocapitalism, with a mesmerizing imaging machine in thrall to the compositional and chromatic elements of the very framework responsible for our environmental destruction. Far from being alone in this endeavor, Burtynsky's aestheticist version of photography is also taken up by photographer Louis Helbig in his catalogue *Beautiful Destruction* (2014), which provides similarly disturbing and seductive imagery of the Albertan tar sands. For instance, *Effluent Steam (Tu ch'ele t'ok'é helį) (nipiy kā pe sākicowak piwāpiskohk ohci sīpīsis)* (2012), offers an aerial shot of steam rising as warm discharge is poured from a large pipe into a frozen, snow-covered tailings pond. The image, positioned in such a way that the steam appears to rise above the ground toward the bottom of the frame, conveys the mixture of natural and industrial elements resulting from the processing of bitumen (the viscous black hydrocarbon found in the area), as its noxious byproducts merge with the formerly pristine ecosystem of this previously forested area. But here environmental toxicity is transformed photographically into visual splendor.

In his catalogue, Helbig includes a range of essays by diverse commentators on tar sands development, including those from a pro-industry position, such as Rick George, former president and CEO of Suncor Energy and Greg Stringham of the Canadian Association of Petroleum Producers, who stress the tar sands' value in providing energy security for North America, while pundit Ezra Levant describes the pictures to be of "a liberal, peaceful, democratic society" based on "ethical oil," distinct from the "conflict

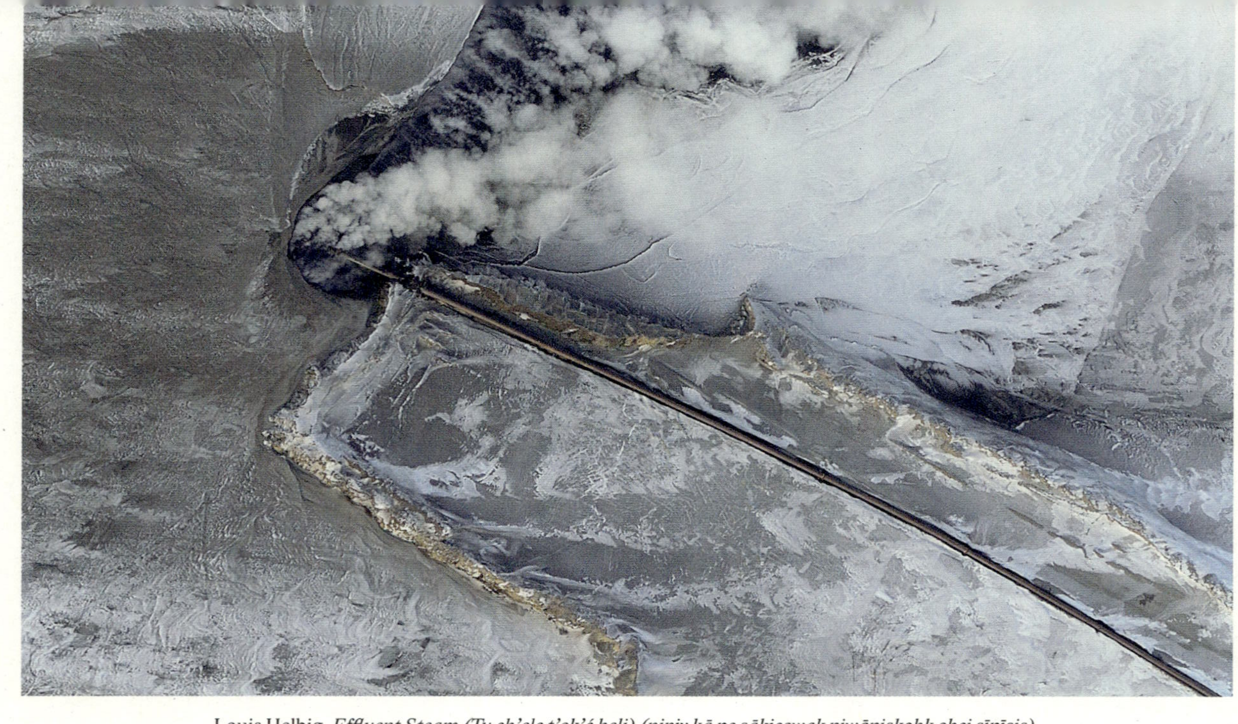

Louis Helbig, *Effluent Steam (Tu ch'ele t'ok'é heli) (nipiy kā pe sākicowak piwāpiskohk ohci sīpīsis)*, +57° 14' 0.59", -111° 33' 10.50, Muskeg River Mine, Fort McKay, Alberta, Canada, 2012

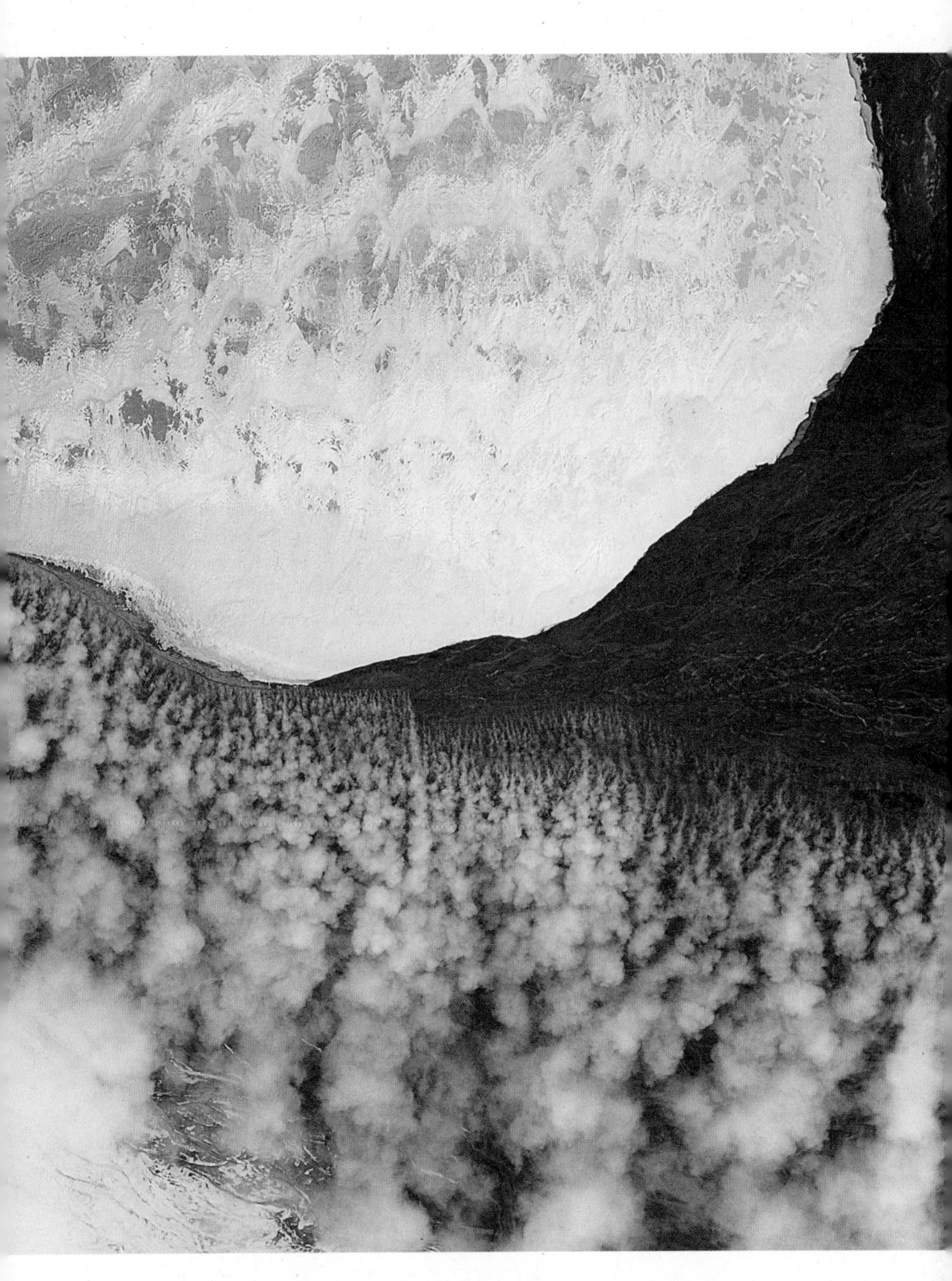

oil" of Middle East dictatorships.[7] There are also critics, including chief Allan Adam of the Athabasca Chipewyan First Nation, who discusses the Albertan tar sands' violation of First Nations rights; Elisabeth May, leader of the Green Party, emphasizes the development's environmental destruction; and Duff Conacher of Democracy Watch highlights the political corruption enabling petrochemical Canada—all speaking to the fact that if "conflict oil" exists anywhere at all it is here. However, it is 350.org founder Bill McKibben's analysis, excerpted from his *Rolling Stone* article "Global Warming's Terrifying New Math" (2012), that offers the most structural account of the link between the tar sands and global warming. He points out that if we were to stay below 2 degrees Celsius (or 3.6 degrees Fahrenheit) warming (as is consistently recommended by the United Nations Intergovernmental Panel on Climate Change), then our worldwide carbon budget over the next thirty-five years is 565 gigatons of carbon; yet there currently exists 2,795 gigatons of carbon in proven coal, oil, and gas reserves, which corporations have *already* factored into their share prices and financial calculations, counting on that money for their current operations.[8] In other words, they possess a massive economic incentive to burn through those reserves, a game-over scenario for a livable climate. It is for this reason that the fossil fuel industry figures as a "rogue industry," in McKibben's terms, and the tar sands, for its extensive environmental destruction, its most visible symptom.

7   Ezra Levant, "This Is What Ethical Oil Looks Like," in Louis Helbig, *Beautiful Destruction* (Victoria, BC: Rocky Mountain Books, 2014), 57, 93. Conversely, analyst Timothy Mitchell argues: "In tracing the connections that were made between pipelines and pumping stations, refineries and shipping routes, road systems and automobile cultures, dollar flows and economic knowledge, weapon exports and militarism, one can see how a particular set of relations was engineered among oil, violence, finance, expertise and democracy." Timothy Mitchell, *Carbon Democracy: Political Power in the Age of Oil* (London: Verso, 2011), 253.

8   Bill McKibben, "Global Warming's Terrifying New Math," in Helbig, *Beautiful Destruction*, 223. For further analysis of the Alberta tar sands, see Jon Gordon, *Unsustainable Oil: Facts, Counterfacts and Fictions* (Edmonton: University of Alberta Press, 2015).

That said, it is not so much the visible damage in Alberta that should be in our focus, but rather the invisible accumulation of greenhouse gases that represents the central imminent threat to the environmental viability of life on Earth. For Helbig, seemingly unconcerned with such invisibilities, photography's greatest value lies in its direct presentation of the world without polemics: "Whatever opinions I might have reflexively harboured as a contrarian, to think and believe that this must be bad, melted into a heady, singular experience of simply responding without editorializing, to just see it for what it is, unfiltered. It was easy to respond with honesty, with integrity to this thing below."[9] The problem is that his images are far from direct and honest. The aerial shot discussed above, for instance, isolates the poisonous industrial exploitation from its larger socioeconomic and politico-cultural environment, thereby transforming it into a putatively innocuous silvery-white composition of painterly abstraction (the photographs of which are then commercialized in editions via art gallery representation and online shopping). The disorienting perspective, cropped and at an angle, produces the sensation of abstract visual pleasure that corresponds to the belief that industry is doing the right thing in Alberta, a result of the fact that Helbig's images were almost all shot from a plane flying overhead, thereby displacing the scene from the misery of those living in or near this industrial apocalypse.

The above whitewashing, if not greenwashing, provides examples of what Nicholas Mirzoeff has called "the aesthetics of the Anthropocene," which, according to his analysis of its nineteenth-century conditions, as evidenced in the Impressionist painting of Claude Monet, "emerged as an unintended supplement to imperial aesthetics—it comes to seem natural, right, then beautiful—and thereby anaesthetized the perception of modern

9   Louis Helbig, "About Beautiful Destruction," in Helbig, *Beautiful Destruction*, 281.

industrial pollution."[10] The logic reminds me ultimately of Walter Benjamin's oft-quoted insight about fascist aesthetics: "Its self-alienation has reached the point where it can experience its own annihilation as a supreme aesthetic pleasure."[11] Is that not what is happening when we admire these images of the tar sands, or of California's oil fields, translating scenes of destruction into compositions of aesthetic beauty? Part of our alienation, in this case, is the perverse enjoyment the photographs afford of images of our own annihilation.

Burtynsky's *Oil Fields*, and Helbig's tar sands photography, can be productively compared and critically contrasted to Richard Misrach's "Petrochemical America," a photo exhibition, and later a book project put together with landscape architect Kate Orff, which hones in on the damaging socio-environmental causes and effects of oil industry development, imaged as a pollution-filled apocalyptic landscape. One photograph, entitled *Abandoned Trailer, Mississippi River, Near Dow Chemical Plant, Plaquemine, Louisiana* (1998), shows the major waterway dishonorably reduced to a sewer, depopulated ostensibly from the toxic emissions of industry historically dumped directly into the water and released into the air. By loading the river with this noxious chemical freight, the petrochemical industry has created an enormous hypoxic dead zone in the Gulf of Mexico, estimated at seven thousand to eight thousand square miles (for which the American Environmental Protection Agency has recently been sued by environmentalists, including the Gulf Restoration Network, for failing to protect).[12]

---

10 Nicholas Mirzoeff, "Visualizing the Anthropocene," in "Visualizing the Environment," ed. Allison Carruth and Robert P. Marzec, special issue, *Public Culture* 26, no. 2 (Spring 2014): 220.

11 Walter Benjamin, "The Work of Art in the Age of Its Technological Reproducibility," in *Walter Benjamin: Selected Writings, 1938–1940*, ed. Howard Eiland and Michael William Jennings (Cambridge, MA: Harvard University Press, 2003), 270.

12 Dahr Jamail, "Environmentalists Sue EPA over Dead Zone in Gulf of Mexico," *Truthout*, August 14, 2015, http://www.truth-out.org/news/item/32354-environmentalists -sue-epa-over-dead-zone-in-gulf-of-mexico.

Unlike Burtynsky's pictorialism, and Helbig's aerial beautification of destruction—and opposite the remote-sensing imagery that tends to fetishize mastery of the visual field as a compensatory maneuver against recognizing the techno-scientific risks of geo-engineering—this photograph rejects the Anthropocene's terminological obfuscations and disavowals of culpability. It shows its on-the-ground environmental and human costs. As such, Misrach's photograph invokes the Capitalocene's insistence on linking geological alteration to the current political economy, showing the "Cancer Alley" of Southern oil development as part of petrocapitalism's necropolitics of ecocide.[13] It thereby inspires criticality and encourages viewers to participate in the growing opposition to fossil-fuel extractivism and its unevenly distrusted effects—a political (and politicizing) relationality otherwise absent in Anthropocene discourse.

Misrach shot his images of the 150-mile Mississippi River corridor between Baton Rouge and New Orleans in 1998 at the invitation of the High Museum in Atlanta (for its exhibition "Picturing the South"). He was subsequently joined by Orff, along with her New York–based firm SCAPE, to collaborate on the photo book *Petrochemical America* (2012), reprinting the original photographic series along with Orff's "Ecological Atlas," the latter providing a stunning analysis of the industrial, economic, sociopolitical, and ecological conditions that frame the "petrolized" landscapes Misrach's images depict. For instance, one of Orff's diagrams links an assortment of chemicals—such as isopropylamine, methanol, melamine, and polyisobutylene—to the places along the Mississippi where they are produced by corporations like Monsanto, Shell, Union

---

13   With this phrase, I reference Achille Mbembe's discussion of the colonial governmentality of death in "Necropolitics," *Public Culture* 15, no. 1 (Winter 2003): 11–40; and link it to Polly Higgins's legal defense against the destruction of natural environments, in *Eradicating Ecocide: Exposing the Corporate and Political Practices Destroying the Planet and Proposing the Laws Needed to Eradicate Ecocide* (London: Shepheard-Walwyn, 2010).

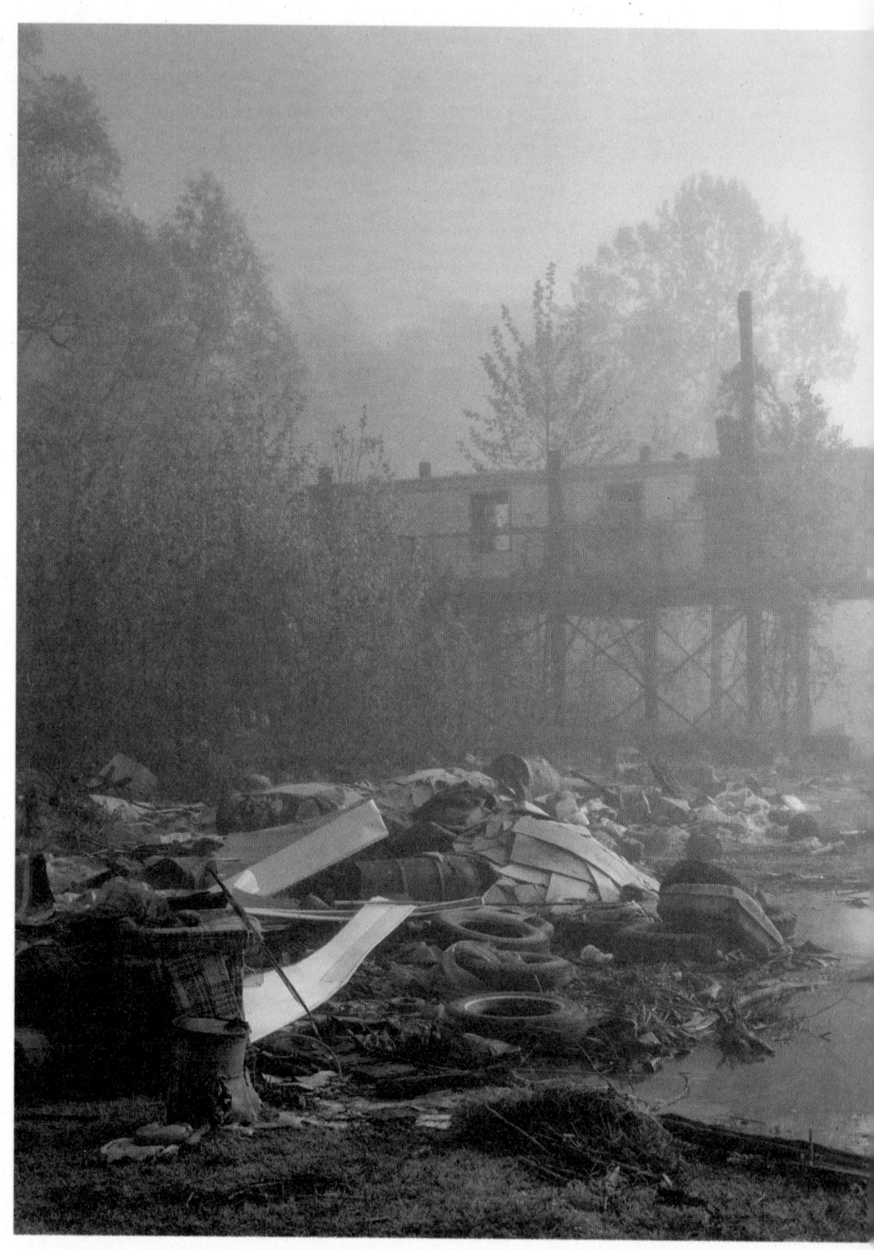

Richard Misrach, *Abandoned Trailer, Mississippi River, near Dow Chemical Plant, Plaquemine, Louisiana*, 1998

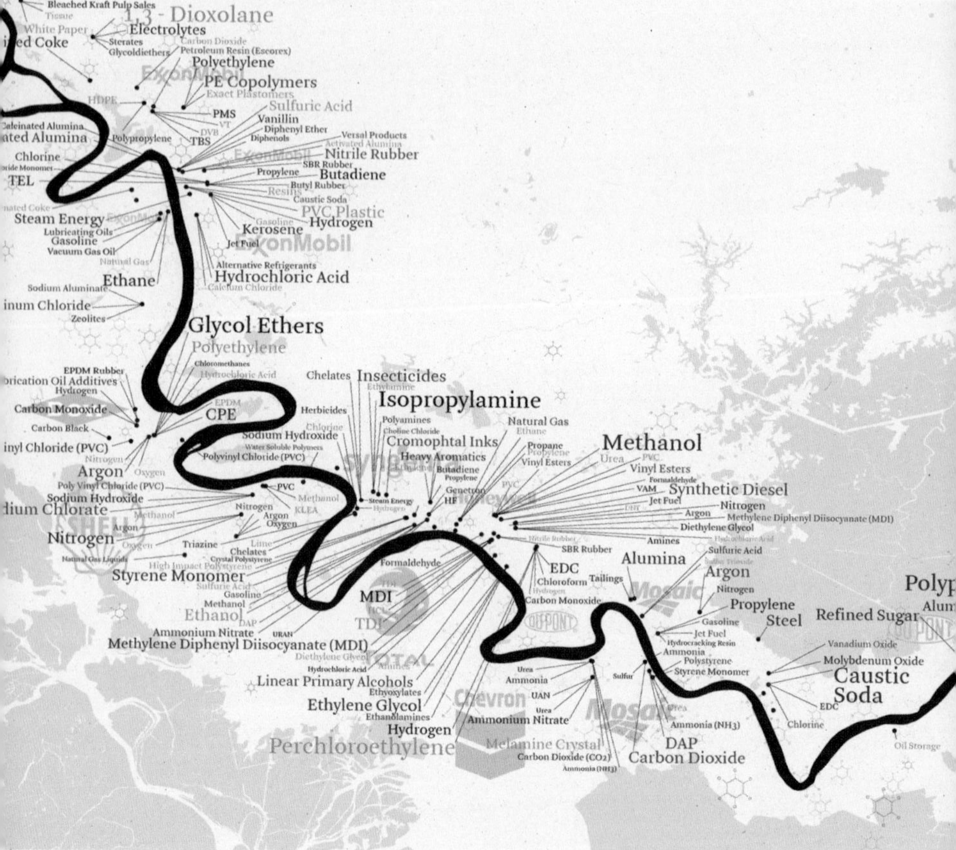

SCAPE Landscape Architecture, *Petrochemical Landscape*, 2012

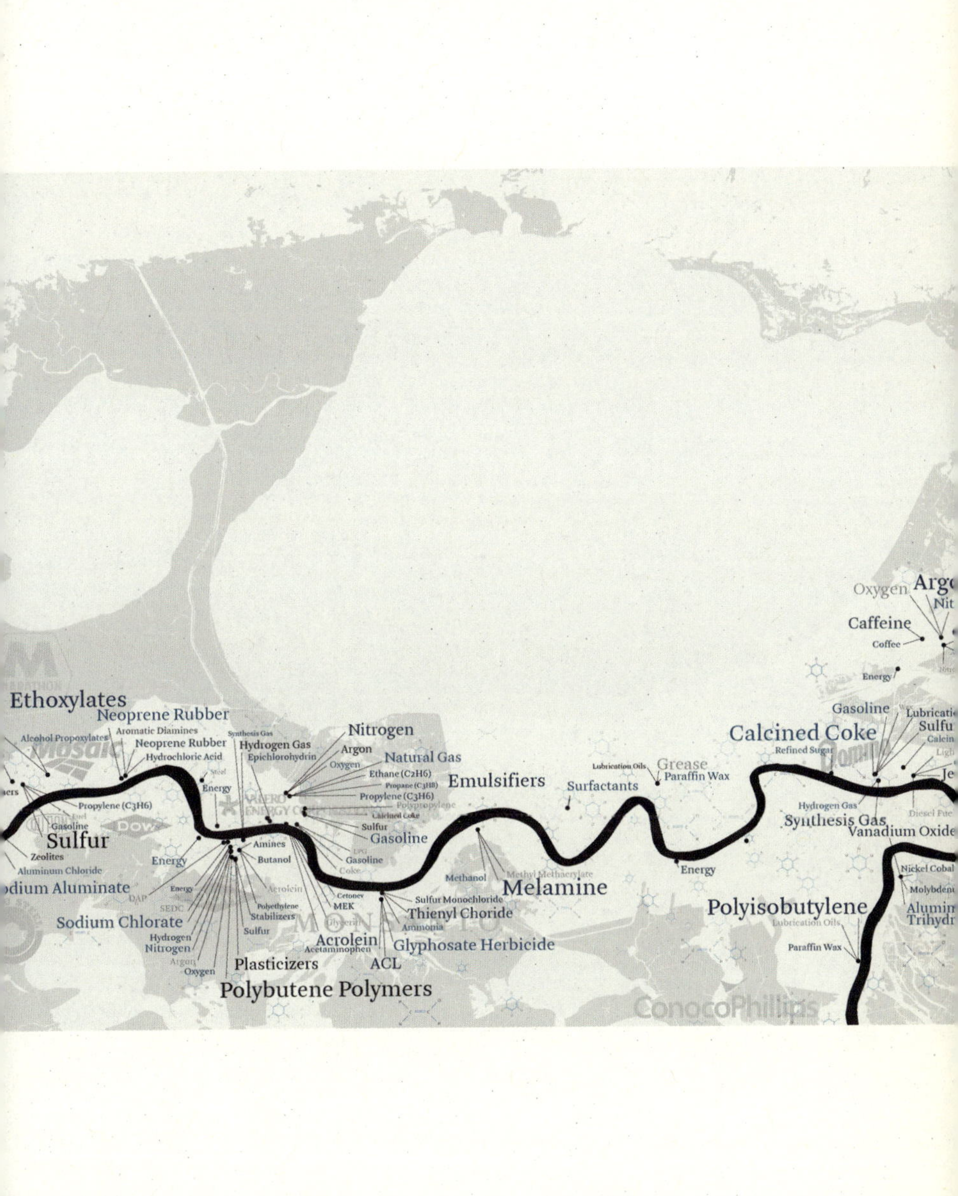

Oxygen
Argo
Nit
Caffeine
Coffee
Energy
Gasoline
Lubricatio
Calcined Coke
Sulfu
Calcin
Refined Sugar
Light
Je
Ethoxylates
Neoprene Rubber
Aromatic Diamines
Alcohol Propoxylates
Neoprene Rubber
Synthesis Gas
Hydrochloric Acid
Hydrogen Gas
Epichlorohydrin
Nitrogen
Argon
Oxygen
Natural Gas
Ethane (C2H6)
Propane (C3H8)
Propylene (C3H6)
Polypropylene
Emulsifiers
Lubrication Oils
Grease
Paraffin Wax
Surfactants
Hydrogen Gas
Synthesis Gas
Steel
Energy
Propylene (C3H6)
Gasoline
Fuel
Calcined Coke
Sulfur
Gasoline
Vanadium Oxide
Diesel Fue
Sulfur
Zeolites
Amines
LPG
Gasoline
Energy
Butanol
Gasoline
Coke
Nickel Cobal
Aluminum Chloride
Methanol
Methyl Methacrylate
Molybden
dium Aluminate
Energy
Acrolein
Cetonev
Sulfur Monochloride
Melamine
Polyisobutylene
Alumin
Trihydr
Sodium Chlorate
SEDC
Pobethylene
MEK
Thienyl Choride
Lubrication Oils
Stabilizers
Glycerin
Ammonia
Paraffin Wax
Hydrogen
Sulfur
Acrolein
Glyphosate Herbicide
Nitrogen
Acetaminophen
Argon
Plasticizers
ACL
Oxygen
Polybutene Polymers
ConocoPhillips

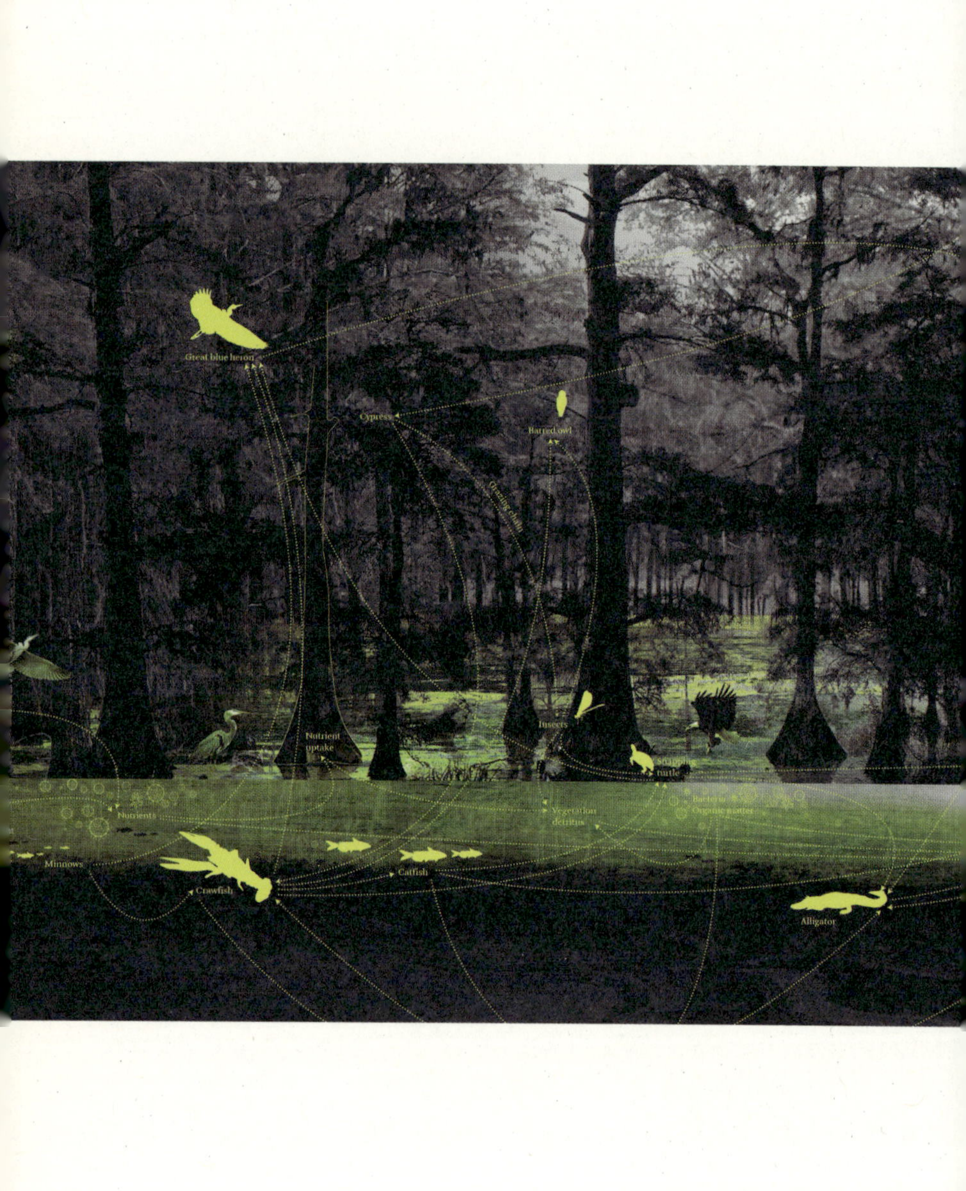

Great blue heron
Cypress
Barred owl
Grazing chain
Nutrient uptake
Insects
Snapping turtle
Bacteria
Organic matter
Nutrients
Vegetation detritus
Minnows
Catfish
Crawfish
Alligator

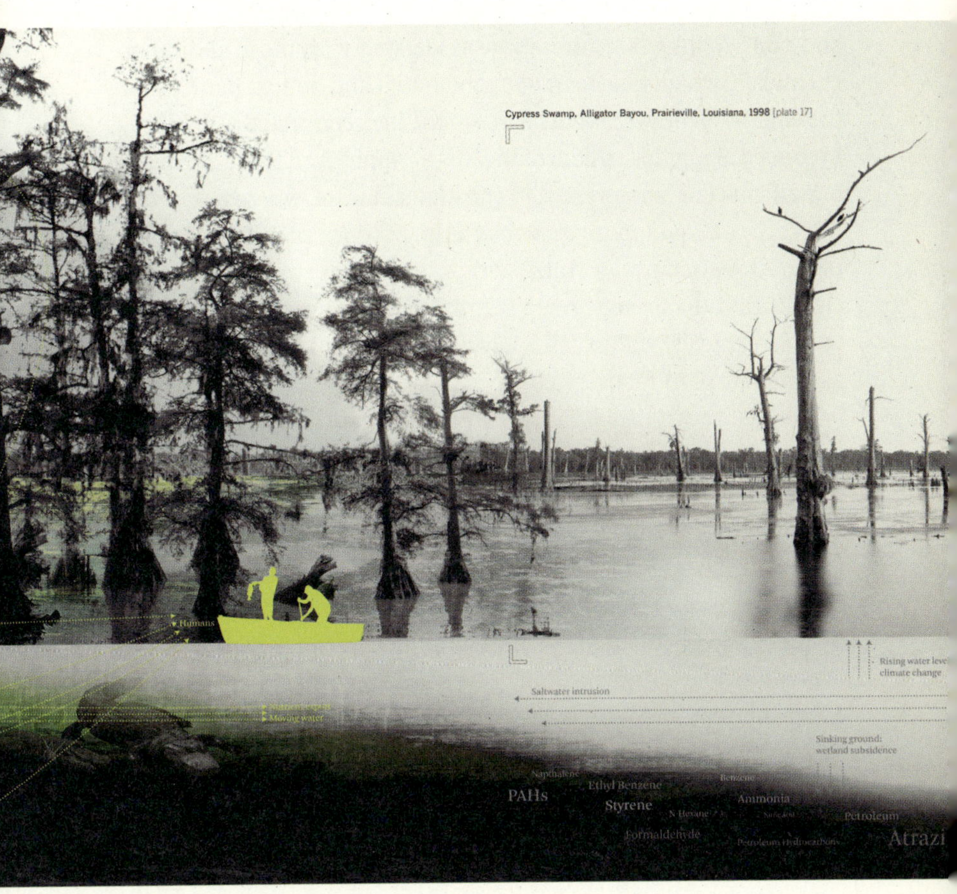

SCAPE Landscape Architecture, *Requiem for Bayou*, 2012

Carbide, Syngenta, Exxon, and Dow Chemical, providing a detailed infoscape that usefully footnotes and contextualizes Misrach's photographs. Other images catalogue the health problems—including cancer, endocrine disruption, premature birth, leukemia, asthma, and non-Hodgkin's lymphoma—associated with those and other chemicals, which bioaccumulate in animal and human bodies and the environment, wreaking havoc on the interconnected web of life. Produced along this stretch of the Mississippi River, those chemical ingredients are omnipresent in consumer culture, where fossil-fuel derivatives help bind together clothing, produce cars, tires, manufactured seat covers, fertilize corn, make product packaging and cleaning products, and create pharmaceuticals and cosmetics—all paid for typically with plastic polyvinyl chloride-based credit cards, as Orff and SCAPE observe.[14]

Still, Cancer Alley impacts certain populations more than others, which Misrach's images and Orff's texts make clear. Formerly enslaved low-income African-American and working-class white communities, without resources to move to cleaner areas or lacking the resolve to abandon their homes, bear the brunt of petrochemical exposure, while corporations enrich distant shareholders living safely in clean, affluent environments. Injustice builds on inequality. These former communities are the tragically absented in Misrach's spectro-poetics, his stagings of the ghostly disappeared, images that pay attention to the invisibilities of the zones shaped by the entanglement of racial, economic, and environmental violence. In this regard, if forced to retain the term Anthropocene, we might consider qualifying it, given the violence of its differential impacts, its inequality and injustice, as *Mis*anthropocene, making it more descriptive and accurate. Or, as Mirzoeff suggests, let us take into account the term's colonial and genocidal roots, carried over

14   Kate Orff and SCAPE, "Ecological Atlas," in *Petrochemical America* (New York: Aperture Foundation, 2012), 127.

into contemporary forms of environmental injustice: "It's not the Anthropocene, it's the White Supremacy Scene," which amplifies Klein's point in the language of #BlackLivesMatter.[15]

Comprising maps, informational diagrams, and flow charts, the "Ecological Atlas" of *Petrochemical America* also visually integrates Misrach's photographs, offering a remarkable opening up of the pictures, unfolding their visuality to rich politico-ecological interpretation. And it is not only human communities that the project investigates, but also their connection to the region's wider web of life. The dead stumps of once-lush evergreen trees, for example, as shown in Misrach's *Cypress Swamp, Alligator Bayou, Prairieville, Louisiana* (1998), are integrated into Orff's *Requiem for a Bayou*, which schematizes on its left side how the polluted wasteland was formerly a vibrant ecosystem, linking alligators to blue herons, barred owls to crawfish, which supported Cajun fishing communities—a vibrant and complexly inter-joined habitat now devastated by industrial ecocide: "The disappearance of old-growth cypress trees and the linear scars of pipes and canals are only the most visible signs of distress [...] regional aquatic systems and human livelihoods are under threat."[16]

In view of this incredible devastation, Orff rightly wonders if the local environmental justice movement that has grown in opposition to the petrochemical industry in this area is now out of date, given the fact that such development has expanded worldwide, with Cancer Alleys proliferating in places like Russia, China, India, Mexico, Brazil, Nigeria, and Myanmar, as shown in another of

---

15   Nicholas Mirzoeff, "It's Not the Anthropocene, It's the White Supremacy Scene, or, the Geological Color Line," in *After Extinction*, ed. Richard Grusin (Minneapolis: University of Minnesota Press, forthcoming, 2017). Or, as Simon Lewis and Mark Maslin put it, less polemically, "The Orbis spike implies that colonialism, global trade and coal brought about the Anthropocene. Broadly, this highlights social concerns, particularly the unequal power relationships between different groups of people, economic growth, the impacts of globalized trade, and our current reliance on fossil fuels." Lewis and Maslin, "Defining the Anthropocene," 177.

16   Orff and SCAPE, "Ecological Atlas," 171.

Orff's diagrams.[17] Without discounting local resistance, she and her associates at SCAPE advocate for a bioregional, and indeed globally interlinked, comprehensive approach directed toward a post-petrochemical culture of sustainability. Among the diverse practices and concrete policy proposals detailed in Orff and SCAPE's "Glossary of Terms and Solutions for a Post-petrochemical Culture" attached to the back of *Petrochemical America*, are suggestions for citizen action networks, green chemistry, sustainable agriculture, ecological land use, public transportation, and environmental law. The solutions would reject the "linear, mechanistic narrative of endless growth based on extracted hydrocarbons and distributed waste in favor of looped and living paradigms centered on human energy and renewable resources."[18]

Against the backdrop of the environmental justice campaigns and activism discussed here and in previous chapters, one might question the methodology of the Anthropocene Observatory, a project by Territorial Agency (John Palmesino and Ann-Sofi Rönnskog) in collaboration with artist Armin Linke and curator Anselm Franke. Presented at the Haus der Kulturen der Welt, Berlin, in 2013, among other exhibition venues, the piece investigates the genealogy of the Anthropocene thesis, focusing on the scientifico-mathematical calculations of global processes that alter Earth-systems, and archives its findings in the form of texts and videos shown in galleries and on websites. As Palmesino explains in an interview in the book *Architecture in the Anthropocene*, the

---

17   Ibid., 191; see also 166–67.

18   "This companion booklet, the Glossary of Terms and Solutions for a Post-Petrochemical Culture, collects anecdotes, strategies, and case studies that demonstrate how change is happening and how to get involved. No example is a silver bullet. Some are controversial, some whimsical. All help shift away from our collective dependency on fossil fuels. Each offers a solution that we can choose individually, participate in collectively, or pressure our government to implement." Kate Orff and SCAPE, "Glossary of Terms and Solutions for a Post-petrochemical Culture," pamphlet insert in *Petrochemical America*. Also see the proposals of the Petrocultures Research Group as presented in their book *After Oil* (Morgantown: West Virginia University Press, 2016).

Anthropocene Observatory practices a form of "neutrality" toward its subject, a "politics of non-action"—"not to take a position, not to engage with conflicts, not to partake in territorial conditions and the reorganization of factions and parties"—according to which it advocates simply witnessing and studying the unfolding of the Anthropocene.[19] Yet, as we have seen, the Anthropocene itself is far from neutral. As such, I find such calls for neutrality to be inevitably complicit in the very non-neutrality of Anthropocene ideology. If we are to survive the Anthropocene—which is indeed a big if— what we need urgently is more activism, not neutrality, to rescue the democratic political process from corporate oligarchs, to enact a just transition beyond the fossil fuel economy, to reassert the priorities of equality, and to eliminate discrimination and prejudice. Whatever we do, we cannot sit back passively and witness our own destruction as a source of either visual pleasure or neutral observation. What is required is "a revolt against brutality," against the violence of climate change—and the language that perpetuates it—as Solnit contends, not the neutral observation of the fossil-fuel-driven destruction of Earth.[20]

19 Quoted in Etienne Turpin, "Matters of Observation: A Conversation with John Palmesino and Ann-Sofi Rönnskog," in *Architecture in the Anthropocene: Encounters among Design, Deep Time, Science and Philosophy*, ed. Etienne Turpin (London: Open Humanities Press, 2013), 23.
20 Solnit, "Climate Change Is Violence."

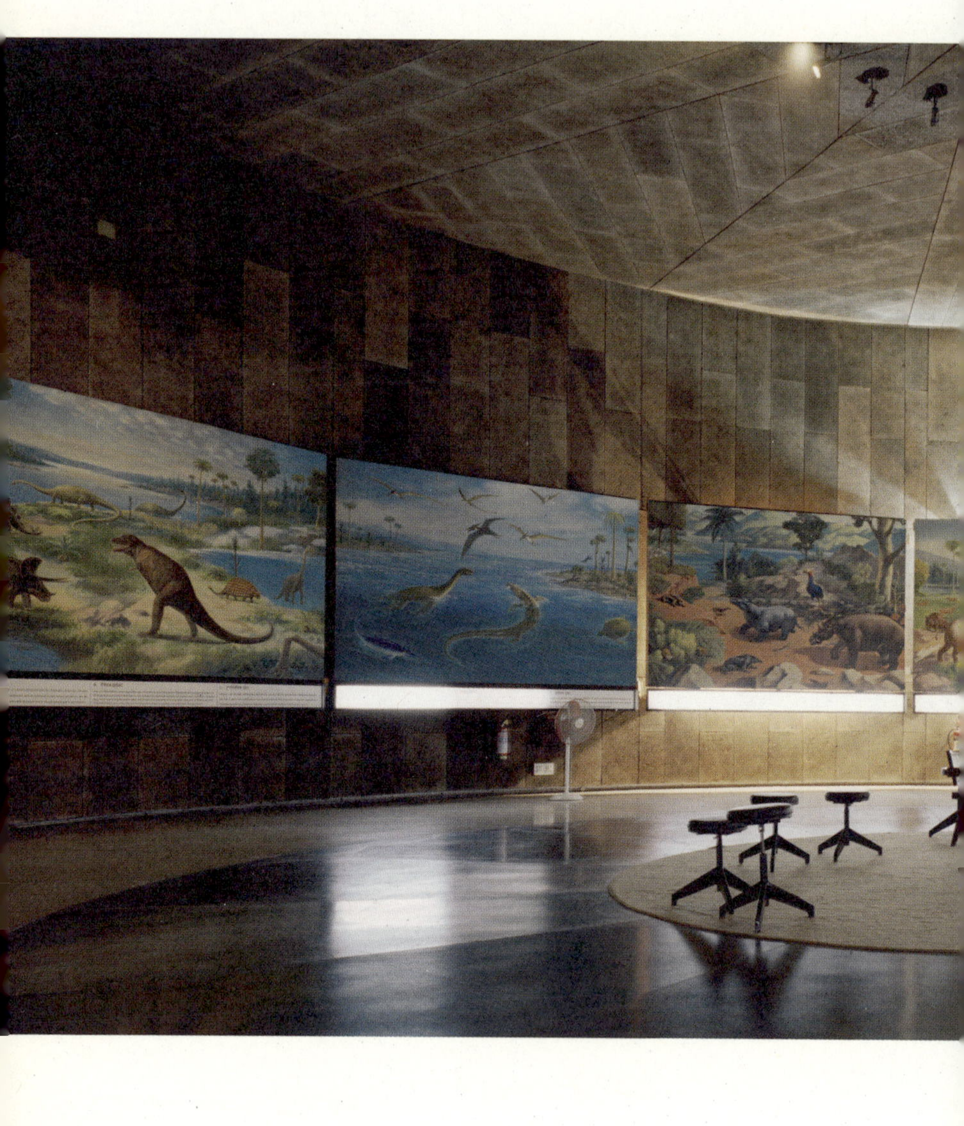

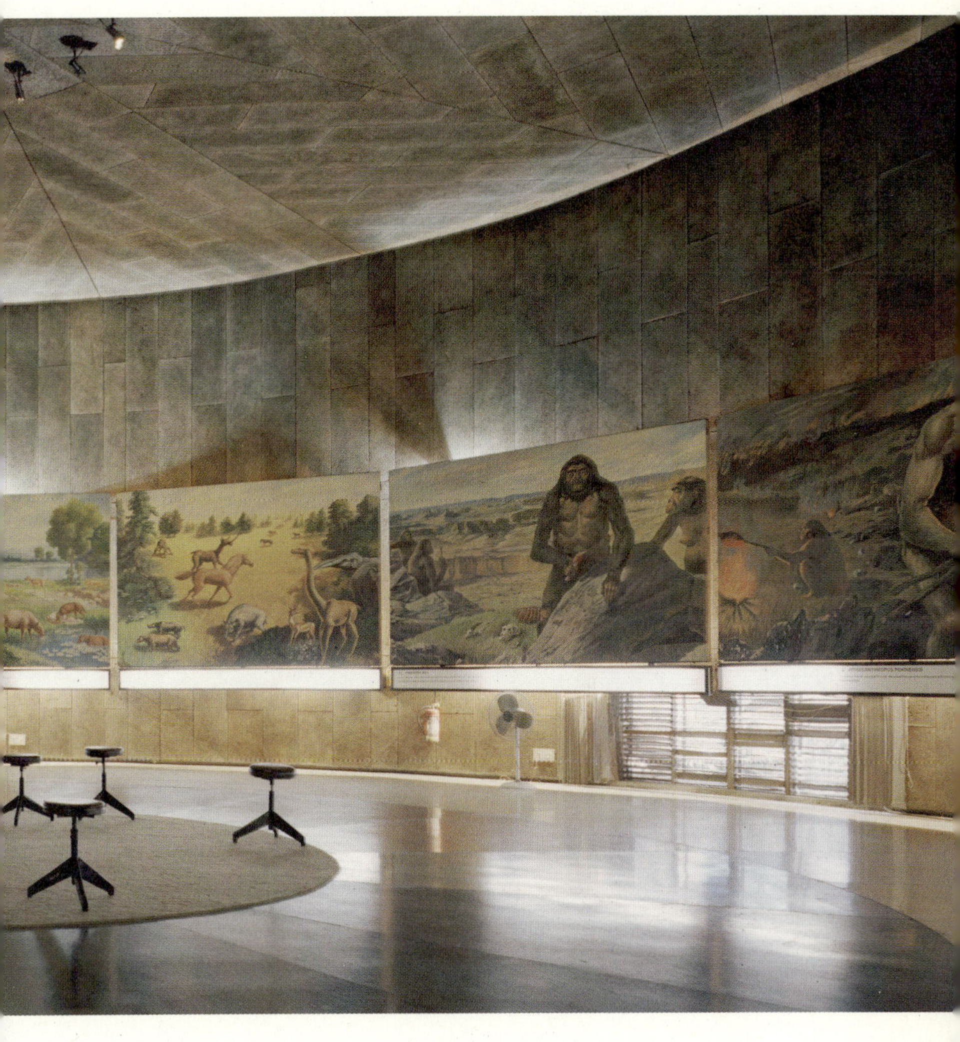

Armin Linke, *Museum of Evolution of Life*, Chandigarh, India, 2014

Chapter Five

Anthropocene, Capitalocene, Chthulucene
The Many Names
of Resistance

In the pages above, we have seen how the Anthropocene thesis can be roundly criticized for its assorted failings—terminological, philosophical, ecological, political. Nonetheless, the term remains significant for one reason: it registers the geological impact of colonial and industrial activities on Earth's natural systems. As such, it offers an important wedge—one that unites climate science and environmental studies with the environmental arts and humanities—against climate change denial, funded generously by the destructive, profiteering fossil fuel industry.[1] And now, with the momentum of its growing adoption across diverse fields of academic, science, cultural, and artistic practice, the term Anthropocene is likely here to stay (and will probably be officially periodized by the International Union of Geological Sciences in the next few years). This, despite, or even because of, its use value in generalizing and thereby disavow-

---

1 See Naomi Oreskes, *Merchants of Doubt: How a Handful of Scientists Obscured the Truth on Issues from Tobacco Smoke to Global Warming* (New York: Bloomsbury Press, 2010); and more specifically Suzanne Goldenberg, "ExxonMobil Gave Millions to Climate-Denying Lawmakers Despite Pledge," *Guardian*, July 15, 2015, https://www.theguardian.com/envi ronment/2015/jul/15/exxon-mobil-gave-millions-climate-denying-lawmakers.

ing responsibility for Earth-systems disruption, validating further geoengineering experiments, and diffusing political traction in the struggle against climate change.

There are of course other contenders for geopolitical descriptors, and among these the leader, in my view, is the Capitalocene—the age of capital—which, as we have seen, has the advantage of naming the culprit, sourcing climate change not in species being, but within the complex and interrelated processes of the global-scale, world-historical, and politico-economic organization of modern capitalism stretched over centuries of enclosures, colonialisms, industrializations, and globalizations. Considering its fifteenth-century origins, Nicholas Mirzoeff writes that "the Anthropocene began with a massive colonial genocide."[2] Yet why retain the term at all? The Capitalocene thesis, by contrast, foregrounds how capitalism evolved within and against nature's web of life, as well as brought ecological transformations to it. In other words, the crisis of climate change, according to this perspective, owes not simply to a substance like oil or coal, or to a chemical element like carbon—and certainly not to humanity's species being—but to complex socio-economic, political, and material operations, involving classes and commodities, imperialisms and empires, and biotechnology and militarism.[3] Of course there have been other economic systems that have also committed massive environmental destruction—such as Soviet Communism, which attempted to force nature into submission at enormous human and ecological expense—but those examples are now historically concluded or transformed into authoritarian market economies, so that we now confront the unavoidable globalization of neoliberal capital, which puts the Capitalocene front and center. This terminological choice is not simply a matter

<hr>

2   Mirzoeff, "It's Not the Anthropocene," 17.
3   See Jason W. Moore, "The Capitalocene, Part I: On the Nature & Origins of Our Ecological Crisis," June 2014, http://www.jasonwmoore.com/uploads/The_Capitalocene__Part_I __June_2014.pdf.

of semantics, but of historical truth, as well as prospective and transformative justice—to pursue an effective transition toward a post-fossil fuel future that is socially and politically just, and to create a common world in which all will not be blamed for the activities of the few, and where culpability for ecocide is assigned to those responsible so that the future becomes not only possible but guaranteed.

That said, no doubt we need many names to account for the sheer complexity and multiple dimensionality of this geo-politico-economic formation, as well as to identify effective sources of resistance and inspire emergent cultures of survival.[4] If so, then another readily available candidate is the Chthulucene, a proposal of Donna Haraway's that draws on the resources of science fiction as much as science fact, speculative feminism as much as speculative fabulation, in naming our present age of multi-species intra-actions, non-patriarchal becomings, and generative collaborations. Distinct from sci-fi writer H. P. Lovecraft's malevolent dragon-octopus-anthropos-shaped monster Cthulhu, Haraway's neologism is proposed rather as a name of names with a thick and global mythological genealogy. It references the "diverse earth-wide tentacular powers and forces and collected things with names like Naga, Gaia, Tangaroa (burst from water-full Papa), Terra, Haniyasu-hime, Spider Woman, Pacha-mama, Oya, Gorgo, Raven, A'akuuujjusi, and many many more." As such, the Chthulucene—from the Greek *khthôn*, the chthonic ones, and the "now" of *kainos*—suggests "myriad temporalities and spatialities and myriad intra-active entities-in-assemblages, including the more-than-human, other-than-human, inhuman, and human-as-humus."[5] Such is the post-anthropocentric, non-human-exceptionalist, and post-individualist basis for Haraway's rejection

---

4   See Eileen Crist, "On the Poverty of Our Nomenclature," in *Anthropocene or Capitalocene*, 14–33.

5   Haraway, "Anthropocene, Capitalocene, Plantationocene, Chthulucene," 160, with nods to Lynn Margulis's ideas of "symbiogenesis," Karan Barad's notions of "intra-action," and Bruno Latour's advocacy for the "progressive composition of a common world."

of the Anthropocene's regressive figuration, and equally the Capitalocene's insufferable reality—both, for her, are mired in cynicism, defeatism, and "game-over" rhetoric, or alternately an irresponsible (non-response-able) looking-away techno-utopianism: "The unfinished Chthulucene must collect up the trash of the Anthropocene, the exterminism of the Capitalocene, and chipping and shredding, and layering like a mad gardener, make a much hotter compost pile for still possible pasts, presents, and futures."[6] Contrary to the essentializing figure of anthropos, which assumes the human to be the self-sufficient, singular sovereign of its world, the Chthulucene conceptualization reveals the distributed, entangled, and interconnected agencies involved in climate chaos as much as its antidote: the condition of life's ongoingness. Haraway's language highlights the resilient generative practices of interspecies collaborations and the "sympoiesis" and "symbiogenesis" of co-becoming that determine the very material conditions of existence. While her term shifts the focus away from corporate neoliberalism, neocolonialism, and extractivism emphasized by the Capitalocene thesis, which Haraway nonetheless also draws upon as a critical diagnostic with which to read elements of the present, it has the advantage of outlining the necessary ethics of what she terms "response-ability," the skilled capacities for survival on a damaged planet that comprise so many "ecologies of practice," including interspecies justice, ethical mutuality, and sustainable co-belonging.[7]

Additionally, and not unrelated to the Chthulucene, there is the Gynecene thesis, implying a gender-equalized, feminist-led, anti-anthropos environmentalism, which locates human-caused

---

6   Haraway, *Staying with the Trouble*, 57. See also Donna Haraway et al., "Anthropologists Are Talking—About the Anthropocene," *Ethnos: Journal of Anthropology* 81, no. 3 (2015), where Haraway intones: "Please tell me that you share my anger, that in this moment of trans-disciplinarity and multispecies everything, in this moment of beginning to get a glimmer of how truly richly complex the world is and always has been, someone has the unmitigated arrogance to name it the Anthropocene. [Laughter] Tell me you share my anger!" (11).

7   Haraway, *Staying with the Trouble*, 34.

geological violence as coextensive with patriarchal domination, linking ecocide and gynecide.[8] As the 2015 "Manifesto for the Gynecene—Sketch for a New Geological Era," authored by artists Alexandra Pirici and Raluca Voinea, explains:

> We declare the imperative necessity for a new geological era to be commenced, before the Anthropocene is even officially admitted on that scale (it might be that by the time it gets fully acknowledged, it will be too late). Rather than continue to contemplate our annihilation, contributing to it or declaring hopelessness in front of it, we should at least try another approach—and this approach has to exclude patriarchy in all its expressions and institutionalized forms of violence: domination, exploitation, slavery, colonialism, profit, exclusion, monarchy, oligarchy, mafia, religious wars.[9]

Contesting the ravages of anthropos, and equally the inequalities of capitalist rule, the Gynecene manifesto calls for new models of eco-feminist stewardship, resonating in part with Indigenous postcolonial reverence for Mother Earth, or Pachamama, as set within the multifaceted rights-of-nature mobilizations in South America.[10]

8   According to my research, the first usage of the term "Gynecene" online was *Le forum TRANS—Rencontres transgenres—Transsexualité (s)*, April 11, 2010, http://www.i-trans .net/forum-trans/viewtopic.php?f=3&t=11604&start=50&view=print (referred to in this source as Gynocene).

9   Alexandra Pirici and Raluca Voinea, "Manifesto for the Gynecene—Sketch for a New Geological Era," *tranzit.ro*, January 2015, http://ro.tranzit.org/file/MANIFESTO-for-the-Gynecene.pdf.

10   Benjamin Dangl, "The Politics of Pachamama: Natural Resource Extraction vs. Indigenous Rights and the Environment in Latin America," *Upside Down World*, April 25, 2014, http:// upsidedownworld.org/main/international-archives-60/4816-the-politics-of-pachamama -natural-resource-extraction-vs-indigenous-rights-and-the-environment-in-latin-america. See also T. J. Demos, "Rights of Nature: The Art and Politics of Earth Jurisprudence," catalogue essay for the exhibition "Rights of Nature: Art and Ecology of the Americas" at Nottingham Contemporary in 2015, http://www.nottinghamcontemporary.org/sites/default /files/Rights%20of%20Nature%20The%20Art%20and%20Politics%20of%20Earth%20 Jurisprudence.pdf.

There, the generally benign Indigenous practices of living and cultivating the forests, lands, and rivers over more than thirteen thousand years contrast with the natural-cultural plunder practiced by globally networked, high-tech, colonial, and industrial societies, which, over five centuries of colonialism and globalization have brought the biological, physical, cultural, and human measures of Amazonia to a devastating crisis point.[11] The present movement of Indigenous-led environmentalism is spreading rapidly, evidenced in the People's Climate March in New York City on September 21, 2014, which, drawing together more than three hundred thousand participants, was the largest such demonstration in history. Protesters converged under banners such as Oakland-based artist and climate-justice activist Favianna Rodriguez's *Defend Our Mother* (2014), depicting a Latina-appearing Earth Mother in folk-art style, her head haloed by our flowering planet, its title "associated less with New Age nature-worship than with the Declaration of the Rights of Mother Earth at Cochabamba, or analyses of the 'reproductive labor' of women that bears the brunt of ecological crises in front-line communities," as Yates McKee argues.[12]

The Earth-as-Mother (a figure of the Pachamamacene?) also links to post-heteronormative, ecosexualist care for Earth-as-Lover, as appearing in the carnivalesque Earth-marriage ceremonies of performance artist-activists Elizabeth Stephens and Annie Sprinkle. They deploy matrimony as a radical act against environmental destruction, and Earth-love as a retort to ecocide. As announced in their "Ecosex Manifesto":

We are madly, passionately and fiercely in love, and we are grateful for this relationship each and every day. [...] We are

---

11   See A. C. Roosevelt, "The Amazon and the Anthropocene: 13,000 years of Human Influence in a Tropical Rainforest," in "When Humans Dominated the Earth: Archeological Perspectives on the Anthropocene," ed. Jon M. Erlandson and Todd J. Braje, special issue, *Anthropocene* 4 (December 2013): 84.

12   Yates McKee, "Art after Occupy—Climate Justice, BDS and Beyond," *Waging Nonviolence*, July 30, 2014, http://wagingnonviolence.org/feature/art-after-occupy/.

aquaphiles, teraphiles, pyrofiles, and aerophiles. We shamelessly hug trees, massage the earth with our feet, and talk erotically to plants. [We are] artists, academics, sex-workers, sexologists, healers, environmental activists, nature fetishists, gardeners, business people, therapists, lawyers, peace activists, eco-feminists, scientists, educators, (r)evolutionaries, critters and other entities from diverse walks of life. [...] Ecosexuals can be GLBTQI, heterosexual, asexual, and/or Other. [...] We will save the mountains, waters and skies by any means necessary, especially through love, joy and our powers of seduction.[13]

With their film *Goodbye Gauley Mountain: An Ecosexual Love Story* (2013), Stephens and Sprinkle mobilize documentary cinematic practice to investigate devastating mountaintop removal mining and extremely polluting coal extraction in West Virginia, where Stephens grew up. Shown smelling flowers, massaging river stones, lasciviously licking and hugging trees, bathing nude and luxuriating in mud, the artists' joyful celebration of the natural world—where nature figures as an awe-inspiring site of queer becoming and radical indeterminacy, rather than any kind of essentialist ideal form[14]—is nothing but infectious, even if their film is also alarming in its unswerving documentary exposure of industrial exploitation. Stephens and Sprinkle juxtapose anti-mining civil disobedience, unexpected alliance formation, and inspiring activist community-building, to the horrific blasting of mountain tops, the ecocidal destruction of streams and aquifers, and testimonies of corporate deceit, their loving ecosexual romance modeling a refreshingly

---

13 Elizabeth Stephens and Annie Sprinkle, "Ecosex Manifesto," *SexEcology*, accessed September 17, 2016, http://sexecology.org/research-writing/ecosex-manifesto/.

14 Relevant here is Karen Barad's reading of nature's "queerness," defining "a lively mutating organism, a desiring radical openness, an edgy protean differentiating multiplicity, an agential dis/continuity, an enfolded reiteratively materializing promiscuously inventive spatiotemporality." Karen Barad, "Nature's Queer Performativity (the Authorized Version)," *Kvinder, Køn og forskning / Women, Gender and Research*, nos. 1–2 (2012): 29.

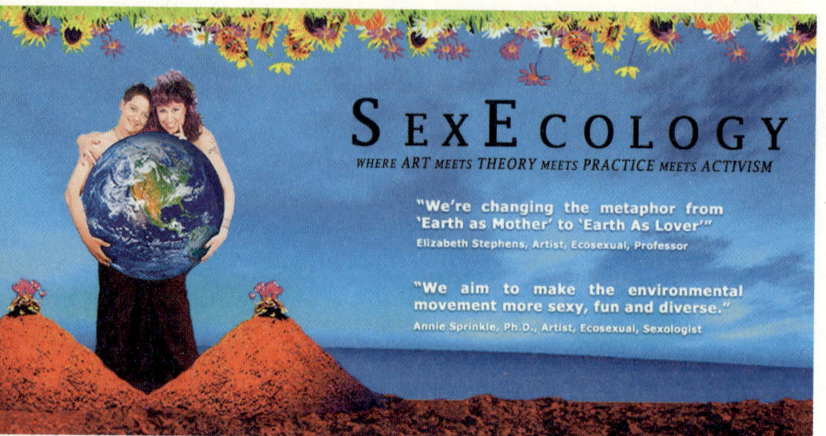

Elizabeth Stephens and Annie Sprinkle with Daniel Wasko Design, banner from the website *SexEcology*, February 2017

libidinal way of being political. In the same vein, and building on Stephens and Sprinkle's precedent, Pony Express, a collaboration led by performance artists Ian Sinclair and Loren Kronemyer, set up *Ecosexual Bathhouse* in 2016 in their home town of Melbourne. The installation encompasses six chambers—including the Pollination gallery, the Composting Glory Hole, the Devolution Swing, and the Capitalcene Sauna—where visitors can engage in "pandrogynous collaborative processes and an antidisciplinary approach to create immersive alternative realities" based on libidinally charged, Chthulucene-instantiating human-flora assemblages, as shown in the installation's documentation.[15]

Another option for names critical and creative, alternatives to the Anthropocene, is the Plantationocene. As a subcategory of the Capitalocene, it highlights the plantation system—and particularly its nexus of corporate colonialism, quasi or explicit slave labor, and the commodification of nature—as a structural cause of geological transformation, from the eighteenth- and nineteenth-century Spanish-mission-led

15   "Ecosexual Bathhouse," *Pony Express*, accessed September 20, 2016, http://helloponyex press.com/projects/#/ecosexualbathhouse/.

colonization of California to the cotton and sugar slave-worked plantations in North and South America of the same era, and from the Belgian rubber plantations in late nineteenth-century Congo to the current sites of biogenetically assisted industrial agriculture in Argentina, India, and Indonesia.[16] The plantation system intensified the oppression of women and the regimentation of normative racial and gender codes, and suppressed interspecies co-becomings and naturalcultural mutualities, as anthropologist Anna Tsing observes.[17] As such, it brings to mind the Homogenocene, the epoch of genetically and industrially induced monocultures, at the cost of mass extinctions, identifying the de-biodiversifying effects of globalization's reduction of nature to the commodity form via corporate-extractivist-strip-mining-oil-drilling-monocrop-planting-dam-building neoliberalism.[18] "The destruction of global biodiversity needs to be framed [...] as a great, and perhaps ultimate, attack on the planet's common wealth," according to Ashley Dawson's recent research on modern species loss, which is reaching a rate of 140,000 species per year, making the current mass species extinction event—an effect no doubt of Capitalocene exterminism—the greatest loss of biodiversity since

16   The "Plantationocene" was proposed during a discussion in Denmark (as part of the Aarhus University Research on the Anthropocene project), in October 2014, related to an issue, at that point forthcoming, of the journal *Ethnos* titled "Anthropologists Are Talking—About the Anthropocene." See Haraway, "Anthropocene, Capitalocene, Plantationocene, Chthulucene," 162, note 4. Among the related literature, see Vandana Shiva, *Biopiracy: The Plunder of Nature and Knowledge* (Cambridge, MA: South End Press, 1997); Vandana Shiva, "Seeds of Suicide: The Ecological and Human Costs of the Globalization of Agriculture," in *The Vandana Shiva Reader* (Lexington: University Press of Kentucky, 2015); Adam Hochschild, *King Leopold's Ghost: A Story of Greed, Terror, and Heroism in Colonial Africa* (London: Macmillan, 1999); and Elias Castillo, *A Cross of Thorns: The Enslavement of California's Indians by the Spanish Missions* (Fresno, CA: Craven Street Books, 2015).

17   Anna Tsing, "Unruly Edges: Mushrooms as Companion Species," *Environmental Humanities* 1 (November 2012): 141–54.

18   The "Homogenocene" was suggested by Kieran Suckling, executive director of the Center for Biological Diversity, in a comment to T. J. Demos, "III. Against the Anthropocene," *Still Searching* (blog), May 25, 2015, http://blog.fotomuseum.ch/2015/05 /iii-against-the-anthropocene/#respond.

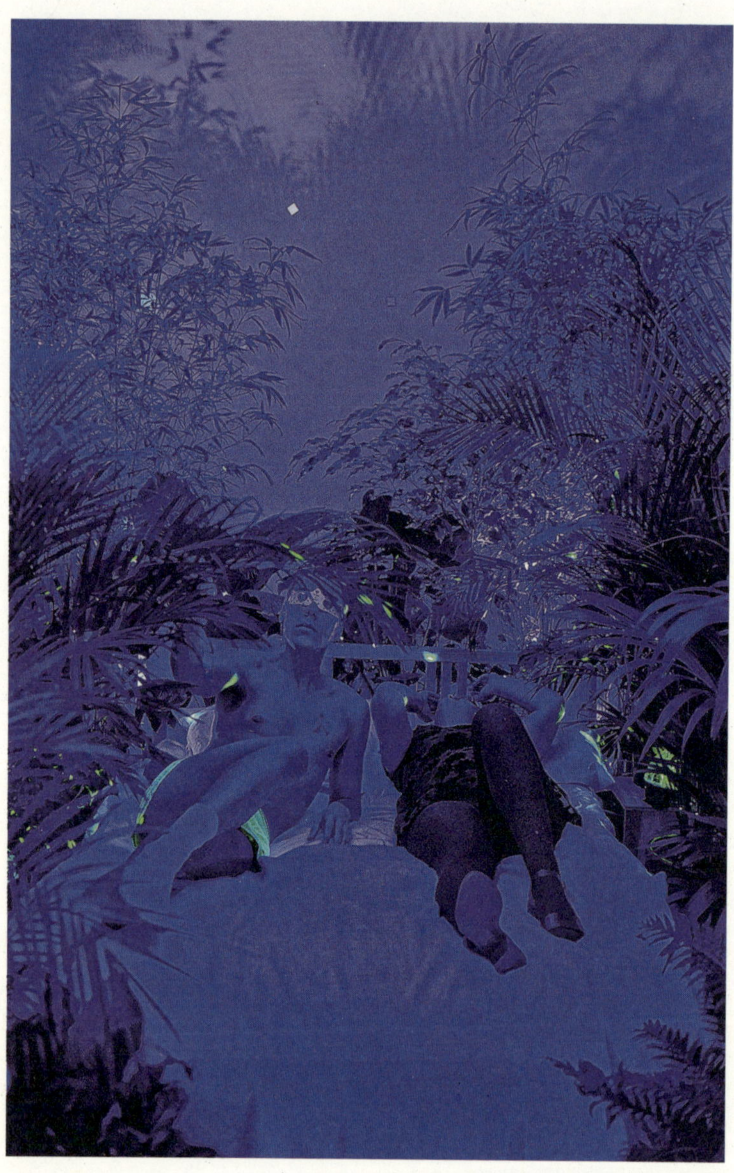

Pony Express (Ian Sinclair and Loren Kronemyer),
Ecosexual Bathhouse, Next Wave Festival, Melbourne, 2015

the Cretaceous-Paleogene extinction event approximately sixty-six million years ago. For Dawson, "extinction needs to be seen, along with climate change, as the leading edge of contemporary capitalism's contradictions."[19]

And finally there is the Plasticene, the age of plastic, which, as Heather Davis argues, figures as perhaps the most exemplary material substrata of living and dying in contemporary capitalism.[20] Indeed, there is so much plastic in our landfills, waste dumps, rivers, and oceans that micro polymer particles—the kind used commonly in toothpaste and cosmetics—have become omnipresent, found to have made a home even in the most remote deep-sea sites before the latter's initial human exploration. We can expect traces of the material to last in the fossil records for millennia to come. Expressive of the fantasy of unending economic growth, the material's seemingly death-defying quality—it takes tens of thousands of years for plastic to dissolve—is made possible by its petrochemical basis, which also indicates the permanency of its environmental devastation. Ubiquitous in consumerist society, its production is only set to grow: while 280 million tons of plastic were produced in 2012, it is expected to rise to 33 billion by 2050.[21]

All of the terms discussed above—and there are still many more—provide urgently needed conceptual tools to test, rethink, and theoretically challenge the Anthropocene thesis. One additional problem with the latter, as we have seen, is what sociologist Jason Moore refers to as its "consequentialist" bias, meaning its tendency to focus on the effects of climate change (global warming, carbon dioxide pollution, sea level rise, drought, etc.), while ignoring the

19   Ashley Dawson, *Extinction: A Radical History* (New York: OR Books, 2016), 13. Also see Elizabeth Kolbert, *The Sixth Extinction: An Unnatural History* (New York: Henry Holt and Company, 2014).

20   See Heather Davis, "Life & Death in the Anthropocene: A Short History of Plastic," in David and Turpin, *Art in the Anthropocene*, 347–58.

21   For further consideration, see Jennifer Gabrys, Gay Hawkins, and Mike Michael, eds., *Accumulation: The Material Politics of Plastic* (Abingdon: Routledge, 2013).

structural causes (what Moore analyzes as the formation over centuries of "capitalism-in-nature" and "nature-in-capitalism"[22]). In this regard, Bill McKibben's recent analysis of climate change's world war appears conceptually misguided and politically questionable: it is not "climate change," or "nature," or "carbon," that is the "enemy," as McKibben's liberal confusion of cause and effect has it, but rather the world historical system that has produced them, which Moore's analysis of capital makes visible.[23] This consequentialist bias also explains why the industrial revolution looms so large in much Anthropocene discourse and in green thinking more broadly, instead of the gradual formation of capitalism's co-becoming with nature, including its colonization of nonhuman and human natures, as in the Americas, beginning in the late fifteenth century, which is its formative stage according to the Capitalocene thesis. As Moore argues, the diagnosis of a problem determines its solution. On the one hand, locating the climate change crisis in fossil fuels, and finding the answer in renewable energies, is ultimately superficial and inadequate—as if we can simply carry on exploiting and colonizing the world, only in new, green ways, and specifically via geoengineering projects.[24] On the other hand, as Moore argues: "To locate the origins of the modern world with the rise of capitalist civilization after 1450, with its audacious strategies of global conquest, endless commodification, and relentless rationalization, is to prioritize the relations of power, capital, and nature that rendered fossil

22   For Moore, capitalism never stood apart from nature but was always internal to it, just as nature provided the milieu necessary for capitalist development. Moore, "The Capitalocene," 5–15. In fact, "Capitalism is not an economic system; it is not a social system; it is a way of organizing nature." Jason W. Moore, *Capitalism in the Web of Life* (London: Verso, 2015), 2.

23   See Bill McKibben, "A World at War: We're Under Attack from Climate Change—and Our Only Hope Is to Mobilize Like We Did in WWII," *New Republic*, August 15, 2016, https://newrepublic.com/article/135684/declare-war-climate-change-mobilize-wwii. For an incisive corrective, see Michael Gasser, "The Enemy Is Not the Climate; It's Capitalism," *Santa Cruz Ecological Justice* (blog), August 22, 2016, https://scej.wordpress.com/2016/08/22/is-climate-change-really-the-enemy/.

24   Moore, "Capitalocene," 4.

capitalism so deadly in the first place. Shut down a coal plant, and you can slow global warming for a day; shut down the relations that made the coal plant, and you can stop it for good."[25]

The Capitolocene proposition locates the origin of the crisis in capitalism's exploitative relations to labor, food, energy, and raw materials. These figure as so many "cheap natures," according to Moore, which, after centuries of exploitation, are now no longer easily available, as there are no more new frontiers and peoples to conquer, only evermore extreme forms of extraction, such as Arctic fossil fuel exploration, fracking for dirty oil, deep-sea drilling, and redoubled but ever-precarious modes of military resource wars and global interventions.[26] This situation leaves us with a choice: either an Anthropocene-Capitalocene future of extreme geoengineering in an age of climate-change catastrophe, ruled by centralist, increasingly authoritative governments and their repressive, militarized police forces alongside ever-heightening forms of socioeconomic and political inequality—this future is foretold in countless eco-dystopian films, the present state of police violence and military brutality (as contested by the international #BlackLivesMatter movement), and glimpsed in the destructive extreme weather events happening already across the world, from forest fires to desertification, melting ice to rising seas. Or, alternately, the formation of re-localized, sustainable cultures based on renewable energy systems, degrowth and redistributive economics, climate justice, regional sovereignty, rights of nature, and new forms of human, even interspecies political inclusion (Chthulucene governance?), and postcapitalist democratic practice.[27] While the latter scenario may seem more challenging than

---

25 Ibid., 5.

26 See Moore, *Capitalism in the Web of Life*, 17; Jeremy Scahill, *Dirty Wars: The World Is a Battlefield* (New York: Nation Books, 2013); and Andrew T. Price-Smith, *Oil, Illiberalism, and War: An Analysis of Energy and US Foreign Policy* (Cambridge, MA: MIT Press, 2015).

27 As Naomi Klein argues, climate change offers "a catalyzing force for positive change," in fact the best argument we have "to demand the rebuilding and reviving of local economies; to reclaim our democracies from corrosive corporate influence; to block harmful new free

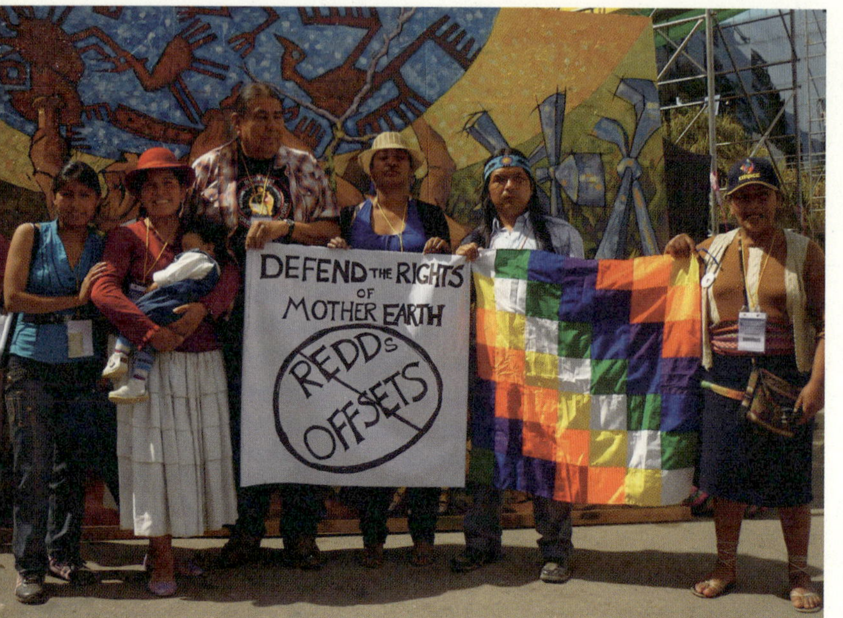

Bolivian demonstration to support the Law of the Rights of Mother Earth, at the Peoples' World Conference on Climate Change and the Rights of Mother Earth in Cochabamba, Bolivia, April 19–22, 2010

ever, and politically beyond reach at present, it is in fact the belief that we can carry on according to the status quo without radical changes to our social, political, economic, and environmental systems that is truly delusional. The goal must be one of hope: to make the impossible gradually possible, for we have no other acceptable choice.

If we were to develop a critical and creative methodology against the Anthropocene, what kind of solutions would its diagnosis make possible? Here I am in agreement with McKenzie Wark: there are no simple solutions to our current predicament—the market will not solve our problems; nor will technology, ethical

trade deals and rewrite old ones; to invest in starving public infrastructure like mass transit and affordable housing; to take back ownership of essential services like energy and water; to remake our sick agricultural system into something much healthier; to open borders to migrants whose displacement is linked to climate impacts; to finally respect Indigenous land rights—all of which would help to end grotesque levels of inequality within our nations and between them." Klein, *This Changes Everything*, 7.

consumerism, or romantic anti-technological primitivism. Rather, we need "to create the space within which very different kinds of knowledge and practice might meet," including "economic, technical, political, and cultural transformations" and "new ways of organizing knowledge."[28] Ultimately, if ecology means relationality, and as such proposes an analogue for a comprehensive politics of intersectionality, then the struggle must be waged on multiple interconnected levels.[29] We must attack new oil pipelines, fracking, deforestation, and all forms of senseless extractivism, as well as target the colonization of nature, violence against women, institutional racism, militarism, and capitalist exploitation. If environmental violence is predicated upon racism and sexism, then racial and sexual reparation must be at the basis of climate justice. It becomes clear, as Daniel Hartley argues, that "at its outer limit, ecological struggle is nothing but the struggle for universal emancipation."[30]

If the Capitalocene sanctions a more directed address of, and intervention into, the processes and causes of current ecological violence, then numerous artistic-activist practices are already providing proposals that insist on embedding experimental visual culture within social engagements and collaborative social movements that are posed against the Anthropocene. They are doing so in order to foster creative forms of life, joining survival to cultural resilience, Indigenous sovereignty to multi-species composition, democratic practice to economic justice and ecological sustainability, which hope to overcome what Haraway provocatively calls the Anthropocene's "killing of ongoingness."[31] Let me identify only a few examples in conclusion.

28 Wark, *Molecular Red*, 22.

29 For elaboration on this notion of ecology as intersectionality, see Demos, *Decolonizing Nature*.

30 Daniel Hartley, "Against the Anthropocene," *Salvage*, August 31, 2015, http://salvage.zone /in-print/against-the-anthropocene/.

31 Haraway, *Staying with the Trouble*, 44.

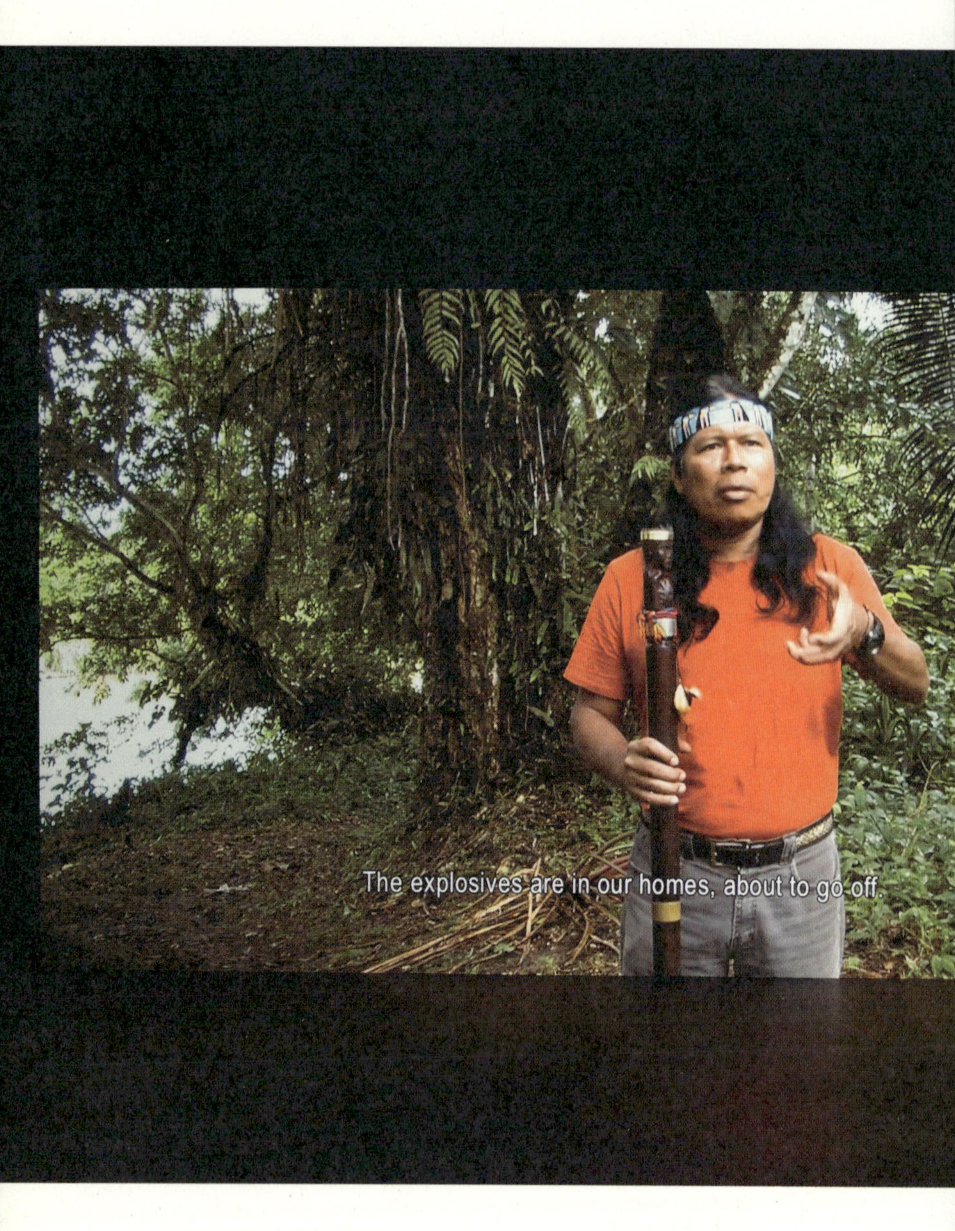

The explosives are in our homes, about to go off.

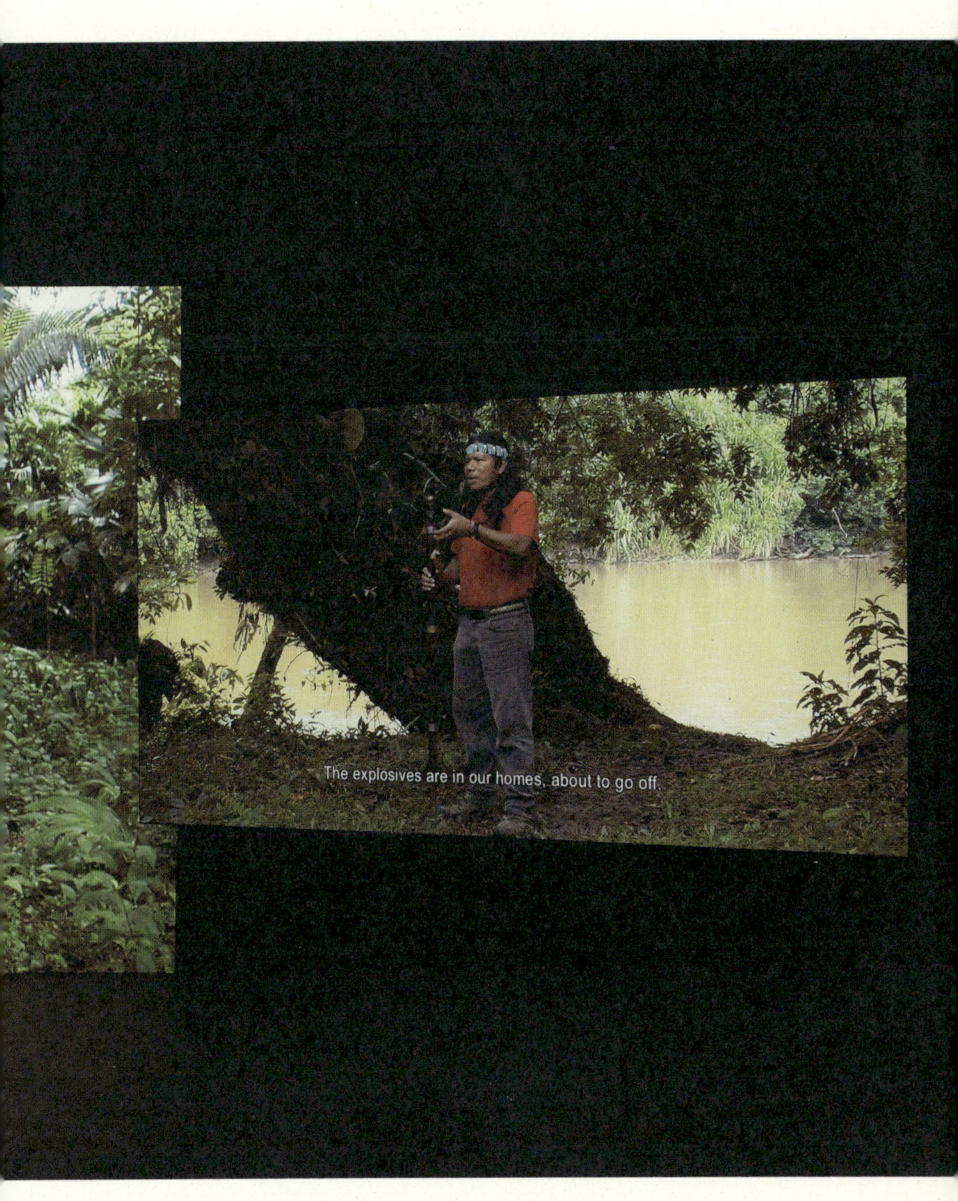

Ursula Biemann and Paulo Tavares, *Forest Law*, 2014

One model is Ursula Biemann and Paulo Tavares's *Forest Law* (2014), a video and mixed-media installation that investigates the history of destructive oil extraction in the Ecuadoran Amazon, Indigenous resistance and environmental activism, and legal proposals for transformative justice. Between 1964 and 1992, Texaco, before it merged into Chevron in 2001, dumped approximately eighteen billion gallons of toxic wastewater in the tropical rainforest (the Deepwater Horizon spill, by contrast, was roughly two hundred million gallons of oil), plaguing local communities with the slow violence of increased rates of cancer and miscarriages, immune system deficiencies, and other serious health problems. The organization Amazon Watch described the pollution as "one of the worst environmental disasters on the planet."[32] Biemann and Tavares's project, which also includes research material presented as a small catalogue, details the struggle of the Shuar and Serayaku for justice through laws—newly enshrined in Ecuador's constitution—that protect the rights of nature. That struggle amounts to a revolutionary juridico-political movement prioritizing eco-centric legality in places like Ecuador and Bolivia, which are the vanguard in what is a growing international formation in Earth jurisprudence.[33] Indeed, Indigenous nations comprise part of the thirty thousand people in this Amazon region who have filed a lawsuit against Chevron in 2001, for which they were awarded $18 billion in cleanup costs and damages in Ecuadorian courts, a sum reduced to $9.5 billion on appeal. While the American corporation has had the verdict overturned in an American court, the Permanent Court of Arbitration in The Hague has recently upheld the Ecuadorian

---

32   Kevin Koenig, "The Chevron Tapes," *Amazon Watch*, April 8, 2015, http://amazonwatch .org/news/2015/0408-the-chevron-tapes.

33   On Earth jurisprudence, see Cormac Cullinan, *Wild Law: A Manifesto for Earth Justice* (Dartington: Green Books, 2002); Peter Burdon, ed., *Exploring Wild Law: The Philosophy of Earth Jurisprudence* (Kent Town, SA: Wakefield Press, 2011); and Demos, "Rights of Nature."

judgment.[34] Investigating this intersection of eco-centric legality, environmental reparation, and Indigenous rights, Biemann and Tavares's *Forest Law* exemplifies the ecological commitments of growing numbers of artist-activists exploring the structural conditions of capitalism's colonization of nature—such as the collective platform World of Matter, of which Biemann and Tavares are both members—and it parallels the growth of transnational alliances in civil society, facilitated by new media ecologies, seeking to establish sovereign and environmental rights from Argentina to the Arctic.[35] In this regard, the project connects to calls for a nonviolent, globally connected, constitutional "climate insurgency," as articulated by Jeremy Brecher.[36] If it is true that we live in a "post-constitutional" juridical present, owing to the corporate intrusion into our legal systems, and the security state's hollowing out of civil rights protections, then we must consider the "moral imperative to revolt" to contest the convergence of growing economic inequality, social and political corruption, corporate oligarchy, police brutality, the criminalization of protest and civil disobedience, and the destruction of the environment, as Chris Hedges advocates.[37]

Another example that reinvents the conditions of visuality in relation to Capitalocene violence is the recent work of Finnish artist Terike Haapoja in collaboration with the writer Laura Gustafsson, which attempts also to realize the cultural terms of a post-Anthropocene form of life. With *History of*

---

34   "The Hague Rules Against Chevron in Ecuador Case," *teleSUR*, March 13, 2015, http://www.telesurtv.net/english/news/The-Hague-Rules-against-Chevron-in-Ecuador-Case-20150313-0009.html.

35   See *World of Matter*, accessed June 9, 2016, http://www.worldofmatter.net; Mabe Bethônico et al., *World of Matter* (Berlin: Sternberg Press, 2014); Demos, *Decolonizing Nature*; and "Thousands Rally in DC to Demand Justice for Ecuador," *Idle No More*, accessed June 9, 2016, http://www.idlenomore.ca/thousands_rally_in_dc?utm_campaign=inmroots8&utm_medium=email&utm_source=idlenomore.

36   Jeremy Brecher, *Climate Insurgency: A Strategy for Survival* (Boulder: Paradigm, 2015).

37   Chris Hedges, *Wages of Rebellion: The Moral Imperative of Revolt* (New York: Nation Books, 2015).

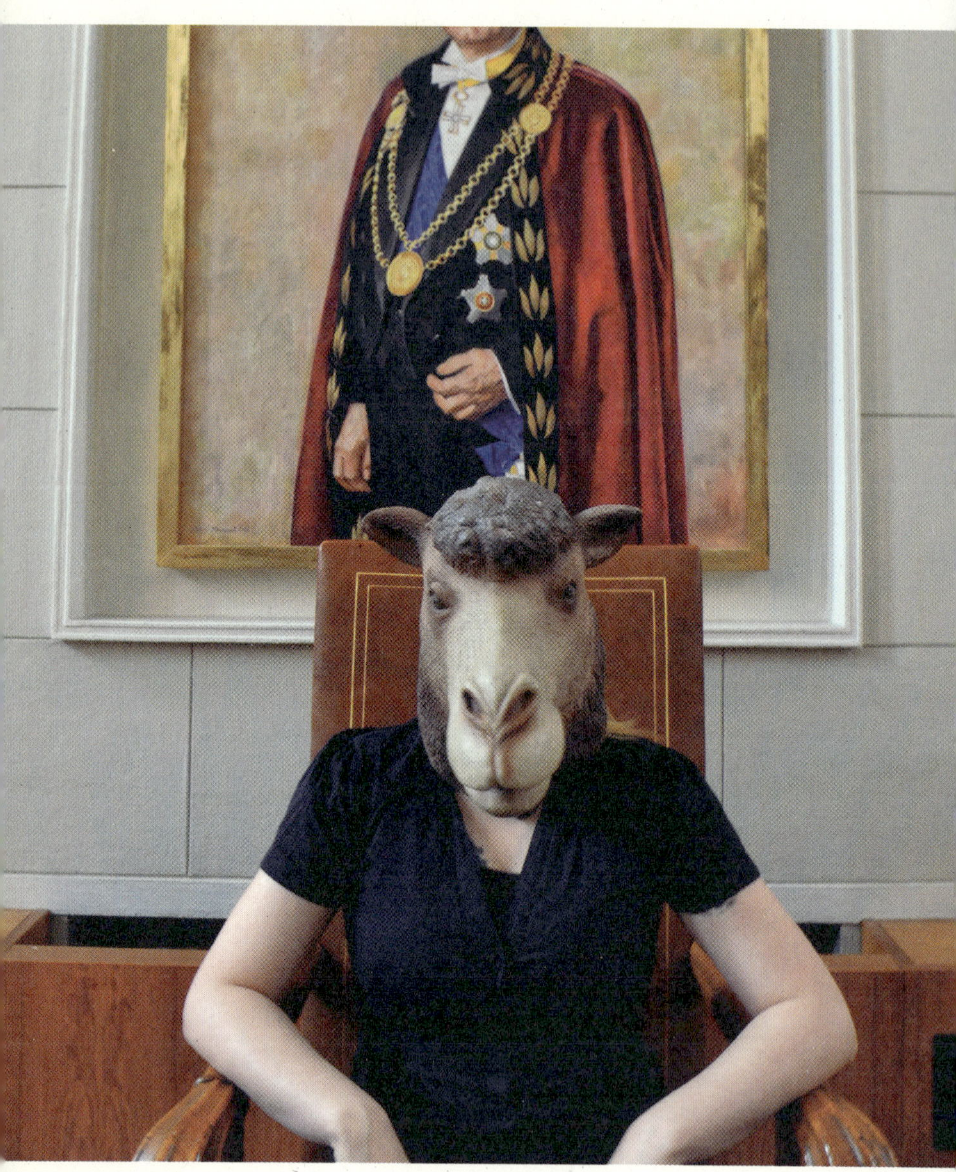

History of Others, *The Trial*, 2014

Others (2013–ongoing), the pair have developed a complex series of proposals for an interspecies cosmopolitics—an alternative post-anthropocentric world-making practice of human-nonhuman relations—mediated by images, performances, imaginary institutions, and diverse social agents.[38] A number of works constitute this project. First, they initiated the *Party of Others* (2011), an interspecies political organization to compete in Helsinki's 2011 parliamentary elections with an expanded human-animal constituency, approximating the terms of what Rosi Braidotti calls "zoe-centered egalitarianism," an inclusive post-anthropocentric legal-political equality among species.[39] Second, they produced the *Museum of the History of Cattle* (2013), assembling artifacts, historical information, and photographic documents presented from the vantage of cows.[40] And third, they modeled a court of law capable of hearing testimony from nonhuman agents such as wolves as well as prosecuting people for cross-species crimes, where hunters can be charged with murder (*The Trial*, 2014). This work may be speculative, but it begins to map the juridico-political terrain of a post-Anthropocene future, a legal-artistic approximation of Haraway's Chthulucene; as such, it prefigures a more just world yet to come.

Lastly, consider Climate Games, a climate-justice action-adventure game initiated by the Laboratory of Insurrectionary Imagination. Based in Brittany, France, the collective (including activist-artists Isabelle Frémeaux and John Jordan) has been working over the last decade at the intersection of climate-justice activism, permaculture gardening, radical-theater practice and pedagogy, and experiments in anti-capitalist collective living. In the fall of 2015, they organized Climate Games to intervene in and contest the

38   See Stengers, "The Cosmopolitical Proposal."

39   Rosi Braidotti, *The Posthuman* (Cambridge: Polity, 2013), 60. For an extensive analysis of Haapoja's work, see my essay "Animal Cosmopolitics: The Art of Terika Haapoja," *Center for Creative Ecologies*, August 2016, http://creativeecologies.ucsc.edu/demos-haapoja/.

40   See the accompanying catalogue Laura Gustafsson and Terike Haapoja, eds., *History According to Cattle* (Helsinki: Into Kustannus, 2015).

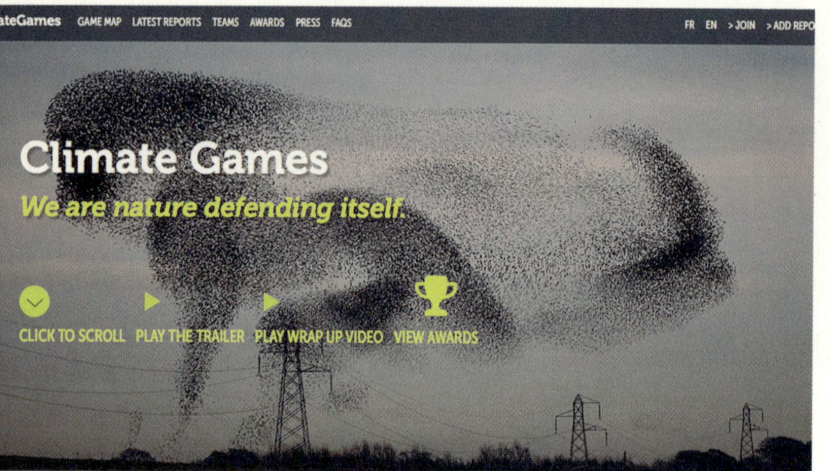

Screenshot of the website *Climate Games*, December 2015

anti-democratic power of multinational corporations in determining the agenda of the United Nations climate change conference (COP 21) meeting in Paris.[41] Climate Games represented a transnational experiment in horizontalist and rebellious movement building, where visual elements, including satellite-generated maps, computerized graphics, cell-phone images, and tactical information, were shared through Internet-linked media networks, all elements supporting and embedded in the movements of insurgent bodies comprising an eco-activist intervention into global climate governance. Working in solidarity with global blockadia movements positioned against oil pipelines and fossil fuel infrastructure, the artwork-as-mass-mobilization invited semi-autonomous participating activists all over the world to coordinate creative political interventions and nonviolent civil disobedience, competing for Climate Games awards by registering and documenting their activities on a networked website.[42] Intended to intensify the joy of disobedience, their modeling of

41   *Climate Games*, accessed June 9, 2016, https://www.climategames.net/ (site currently unavailable).

42   See Klein, "Blockadia," 293–336.

a neo-Brechtian performance of disruption—as well as a kind of neo-Boalian invisible theater that takes place seemingly spontaneously in everyday life—resonated with alter-globalization forces, Occupy, and Spanish Indignado tactics. Frémeaux and Jordan have said, "We need to commit to carry out actions of resistance, of disobedience, to stop this suicidal machine that has literally set the climate on fire and that has lead [*sic*] to the extinction of two hundred species per day."[43] Their Chthulucene-like motto was: "We are nature defending itself."[44]

The achievements of Climate Games were substantial and widespread, even if their effects are still ongoing and difficult to measure: it enabled the international networking of local activist struggles; it generated large-scale media coverage (from the United Kingdom's *Guardian* to Turkey's *BirGün*, France's *Libération* to Germany's *taz*); it introduced radical French movements to creative activist possibilities (as evidenced in the ongoing occupation practices at the ZAD, *zone à défendre*, defending against the airport construction at Notre Dames des Landes); and modeled forms of joyful rebellion that will have a long-lasting influence beyond COP 21.[45]

One amazing convergence of artist-activist energies occurred alongside Climate Games, joining together groups including: the United States–based G.U.L.F., Not an Alternative, and Occupy Museums; the United Kingdom's Art Not Oil, BP or not BP?,

---

43   Quoted in Ewen Chardronnet's interview with Isabelle Frémeaux and John Jordan: "Climate Games: 'We Are Nature Defending Itself,'" *Makery*, May 11, 2015, http://www.makery.info/en/2015/05/11/climate-games-nous-sommes-la-nature-qui-se-defend/.

44   For more on Climate Games, see T. J. Demos, "Playful Protesters Use Art to Draw Attention to Inadequacy of Paris Climate Talks," *Truthout*, December 13, 2015, http://www.truth-out.org/news/item/34006-playful-protesters-use-art-to-draw-attention-to-inadequacy-of-paris-climate-talks.

45   For an overview of participants' responses to Climate Games, see Amber Hickey and T. J. Demos, ed., "COP 21 Questionnaire," *Center for Creative Ecologies*, accessed September 27, 2016, http://creativeecologies.ucsc.edu/cop-21-questionnaire-laboratory-of-insurrectionary-imagination/. Also see T.J. Demos, "The Great Transition: The Arts and Radical System Change," *e-flux architecture*, April 2017, http://www.e-flux.com/architecture/accumulation/122305/the-great-transition-the-arts-and-radical-system-change/."

Liberate Tate, Platform London, Science Unstained, Shell Out Sounds, and UK Tar Sands Network; and Stopp Oljesponsing av Norsk Kulturliv from Norway, creating an international coalition to contest Capitalocene environmental economics and cultural policy. Strategizing together, they held an unauthorized demonstration at the Louvre in 2015, attacking the flagship museum's sponsorship by major oil and gas corporations Eni and Total. The event was particularly courageous given that public gatherings were considered illegal in the context of France's declared state of emergency following the Paris terror attacks half a month earlier, a declaration—particularly anti-democratic in that it allowed the depoliticized activities of shopping and sports games to continue uninterrupted—that threatened to derail all COP 21 protest activities. Outside the museum's I. M. Pei–designed iconic glass pyramids on December 9, performers carried black umbrellas spelling out the words "Fossil Free Culture," and spoke of their support for life beyond petrocapitalism. At the same time, a smaller group created the scene of what appeared to be a small oil spill in the atrium of the museum, and then proceeded to walk through it barefoot and then around in concentric circles, their footprints on the marble floor visualizing the fossil fuel corporations' despoilment of the museum, and more broadly the environment. A number of participants were arrested by the French police and held for a short period for the "degradation of cultural property." But for writer and activist Yates McKee, of G.U.L.F., the police had apprehended the wrong suspects: "The oil footprints mark the scene of crime, implicating the institution in the fossil fuel system and the climate crisis."[46] According to Beka Economopoulos, of Not an Alternative, "On the occasion of the UN Climate Summit in Paris"—the final agreement of which the leading climate scien-

---

46 Lucky Tran, "Artists and Activists Sing, Spill 'Oil' in Anti–Fossil Fuel Protests at the Louvre," *Hyperallergic*, December 9, 2015, http://hyperallergic.com/260399 /artists-and-activists-sing-spill-oil-in-anti-fossil-fuel-protests-at-the-louvre/.

tist James Hansen concluded was a "fraud," owing to its watered-down call for national nonbinding, voluntary contributions to greenhouse gas reductions[47]—"we're urging the Louvre to stop sponsoring climate chaos."[48]

What we witness with Climate Games, and the larger civil society movement of which it formed a part, is a shift in artistic practice toward an activist creativity directed at challenging the very structures of climate governance and finance, including the political economy of cultural institutions. The momentum continues to grow, just as interventions are becoming more bold: earlier in March 2015, Not an Alternative's Natural History Museum project organized "An Open Letter to Museums," signed by nearly one hundred fifty scientists, including several Nobel Prize winners, calling on American museums to "cut all ties with the fossil fuel industry and funders of climate science obfuscation."[49] Generating copious press coverage, the letter was likely a major factor in oil-heir industrialist David H. Koch leaving the board of New York's Natural History Museum in January 2016. An instance of what Not an Alternative has come to call "institutional liberation," its practice moves beyond earlier forms of institutional critique, focused on the critical analysis of institutional functions, and toward emancipation of such spaces from petrocapitalist influence, social and economic injustice, and anti-democratic rule. At about the same time, Liberate Tate and

47   Oliver Milman, "James Hansen, Father of Climate Change Awareness, Calls Paris Talks 'a Fraud,'" *Guardian*, December 12, 2015, http://www.theguardian.com/environment/2015/dec/12/james-hansen-climate-change-paris-talks-fraud. For extensive critical analysis of COP 21, see John Foran, "The Paris Agreement: Paper Heroes Widen the Climate Justice Gap," *Climate Justice Project*, December 13, 2015, http://climatejusticeproject.com/2015/12/13/the-paris-agreement-paper-heroes-widen-the-climate-justice-gap/; and Danny Chivers and Jess Worth, "Paris Deal: Epic Fail on a Planetary Scale," *New Internationalist*, December 12, 2015, http://newint.org/features/web-exclusive/2015/12/12/cop21-paris-deal-epi-fail-on-planetary-scale/#sthash.33wOIPb7.dpuf.

48   Tran, "Artists and Activists Sing, Spill 'Oil.'"

49   See "An Open Letter to Museums from Members of the Scientific Community," *Natural History Museum*, March 24, 2015, http://thenaturalhistorymuseum.org/open-letter-to-museums-from-scientists/.

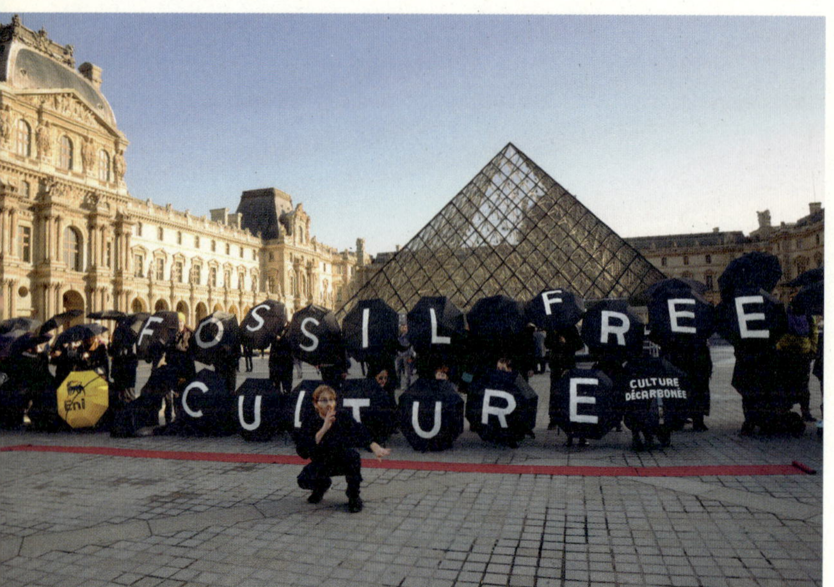

A coalition of international artists and activists stages "Big Oil Out of Culture" in front of the Musée du Louvre, Paris, December 9, 2015. Photo by Sumugan Sivanesan.

other London-based groups won a nearly six-year campaign to compel the Tate to break off its sponsorship agreements with BP, thereby removing the corporation's ability to "artwash" its identity and practice—that is, to make an environmentally destructive business appear as a benevolent cultural philanthropist, and thus securing a social license to pollute.[50] (That said, BP recently announced a new £7.5 million, five-year deal with four major arts institutions in the United Kingdom—the British Museum, National Portrait Gallery, Royal Opera House, and Royal Shakespeare Company—despite all the recent opposition. The struggle continues, no doubt with more activism to come.)[51] The goal of these groups is to reinvent demo-

50   See Mel Evans, *Artwash: Big Oil and the Arts* (London: Pluto Press, 2015).

51   Mark Brown, "BP Sparks Campaigners' Fury with New Arts Sponsorship Deals," *Guardian*, July 28, 2016, https://www.theguardian.com/business/2016/jul/28/bp-sponsorship-arts -organisations-british-museum-national-portrait-gallery. As Anna Galkina of Platform London explained, the deal "would escalate as a result of the renewals. 'BP is ripping off our cultural institutions—their sponsorship provides less than 0.5% of the British Museum's budget. With

cratic self-determination and support fossil-free culture through direct action, by contesting corporate power and its nefarious sway over public institutions. In other words, these practitioners are opposing the current petrocapitalist governmentality—the rule of the Capitalocenologists—that attempts to unilaterally decide how we address environmental crisis, a threat like no other, as complex and interconnected as it is singularly grave and consequential. The artistic element of these actions involves injecting playful theatricality, collaborative energy, and the spirit of positive fun into a forceful wedge striking at the heart of the Capitalocene political economy, revealing the contours of an emergent institutional liberation targeting global climate governance and its cultural normalization.

New media ecologies, climate games, institutional liberation: these are diverse engagements for sure—and there are certainly many more worthy of attention. What they generally share is taking a stake in anti-Anthropocene cultural activism, founded upon the refusal to generalize and depoliticize climate-change agency, and the rejection of current corporate-dominated environmental governance. They each invent creative approaches to alternative forms of life beyond the Anthropocene's techno-fixes and geoengineering ambitions; for these, as we have seen, prefer to address only the consequences, rather than interrogate the systemic and determinative processes of centuries of capitalism's world-historical and colonial co-becoming with nature. As Roy Scranton observes, "if you want to learn to live in the Anthropocene, we must first learn how to die." Learning to die means giving up on "carbon-fueled capitalism and its techno-utopian ideologues [who] have promised infinite growth and infinite innovation, yet [...] have proven incapable of saving us from the disaster they have made."[52]

---

this pocket change, BP buys legitimacy, access to invaluable advertising space, and masks its role in destroying indigenous lands, arming dictatorships and wrecking our climate.'"

52   Roy Scranton, *Learning to Die in the Anthropocene: Reflections on the End of a Civilization* (San Francisco: City Lights Books, 2015), 25–27.

It is precisely such an abandonment of the Anthropocene's ideas, stories, and practices that the above engaged artists have initiated. The transversal connections between politicized collectives and their rebellious poetics disperse, for sure, into countless names—the emergent lexicons of current geologies and potential future epochs now in the making. Whether they will be enough to stop the ravages of near-future catastrophe, even when they join with the power of growing social movements, is another question. But what other choice do we have? In the meantime, the future of Earth hangs in the balance.

Acknowledgments

Many friends, colleagues, family members, and comrades have made this book possible—more than I can name—and I am grateful for all of their ongoing and heartfelt support. The thoughts, realizations, pasts, presents, and futures that this book contends with are no doubt foreboding, but they are also accompanied by moments of hope, glimmering undefeated in the dark. It is one's community that gives meaning to the struggle for a just life, and encouragement to keep going amid troubled conditions. If we stand any chance of surviving the climate-change breakdown that is upon us, we will need such relationships and networks more than ever.

I thank Daniela Janser and Marco de Mutiis of the Fotomuseum Winterthur, whose kind invitation to publish a series of online essays as part of their formidable series "Still Searching: An Online Discourse on Photography" provided the initial opportunity to confront the Anthropocene thesis, out of which this book grew. I have had many opportunities to present early working versions of the present text, and I acknowledge the invitations of my numerous hosts and organizations. The engaged scholarship and critical writings of Subhankar Banerjee, Karen Barad, Ursula Biemann, Heather Davis, Ashley Dawson, Eriel Tchekwie Deranger, Michael Gasser, James Hansen, Donna Haraway, Brian Holmes, Naomi Klein, Achille Mbembe, Yates McKee, Nicholas Mirzoeff, Jason Moore, Rob Nixon, Kate Orff, Rebecca Solnit, Paulo Tavares, Zoe Todd, Etienne Turpin, and Anna Tsing have been instrumental for my own conceptualizations and argumentations, and I express gratitude to them for their important contributions to climate justice, political ecology, visual culture, and anticolonial practice in general. For their friendship, support, and compelling models of practice and writing, I also thank David Joselit, Alex Alberro, Claire Bishop, Terry Smith, Hilde van Gelder, Ros Gray, Emily Pethick, Kodwo Eshun, and Anjalika Sagar.

The artists, activists, and photographers responsible for the amazing and challenging work I discuss all played crucial roles in inspiring my research (even when I take some critical distance), and I owe them enormous appreciation for what they have made possible, while taking responsibility ultimately for my book's inevitable failings and weaknesses. These practitioners include: the Welcome to the Anthropocene project, the Globaïa project, Daniel Beltrá, Chris Evans, Richard Misrach, Kate Orff, Louis Helbig, Edward Burtynsky, Idle No More, sHell No! activists, the Unist'ot'en Camp, the Pacific Climate Warriors, Anthropocene Observatory, Favianna Rodriguez, Beth Stephens and Annie Sprinkle, Pony Express, Ursula Biemann, Paulo Tavares, Terike Haapoja, Laura Gustafsson, Isabelle Frémeaux and John Jordan of the Laboratory of Insurrectionary Imagination and Climate Games, Lucky Tan, Clara Paillard, #FossilFreeCulture, Beka Economopoulos and Jason Jones of Not an Alternative, Jess Worth of BP or Not BP?, and Mel Evans of Liberate Tate.

Many thanks to Marnie Slater's and Mark Soo's incisive editing, Miriam Rech's design efforts, and at Sternberg Press, Tatjana

Günthner's production assistance throughout the publication process and Caroline Schneider's ongoing support.

My partner, Joy Schendledecker, and kids, Zoë Demos and Leila Demos, deserve my deepest gratitude, for reasons only they know. It's painful to consider what future generations—including those of my children—may face as life enters the Anthropocene, and this was a continual motivating thought in writing this book, as well as the conviction that it's never too late for transformation. Let us not falter in our ongoing efforts.

Index

Image Credits

Chapter One

p. 11

Screenshot of the website *Welcome to the Anthropocene*,
accessed October 2016. http://anthropocene.info/index.php.
Courtesy of Félix Pharand-Deschênes/Globaïa.

pp. 14–15

Still from Globaïa's video *Welcome to the Anthropocene*, 2012.
http://anthropocene.info/short-films.php.
Courtesy of Félix Pharand-Deschênes/Globaïa.

p. 16

Global Transportation System map, from Globaïa's webpage
"Cartography of the Anthropocene," accessed October 2016.
http://globaia.org/portfolio/cartography-of-the-anthropocene/.
Information sourced by the International Road Federation,
2011. Courtesy of Félix Pharand-Deschênes/Globaïa.

p. 23

Earth as seen by the Apollo 17 crew, 1972. Courtesy of
the National Aeronautics and Space Administration (NASA).

Chapter Two

p. 27

Aerial view of the Newmont mine, Sumbawa
Island, Indonesia, April 2007. Photo: Sonny Tumbelaka.
© Sonny Tumbelaka/AFP/Getty Images.

p. 31

Graph from NASA, produced in August 2012, documents chlorophyll levels in the ocean off the coast of British Columbia.
Yellow and orange colors in the center of the image reveal unnaturally high concentrations following Russ George's controversial
geoengineering scheme. Courtesy of OB.DAAC-MODIS/
Giovanni/Goddard Earth Sciences Data and
Information Services Center/NASA.

p. 33

Fireboats battle the blaze at BP's offshore oil rig, Deepwater Horizon, Gulf of Mexico, near New Orleans, Louisiana, April 21, 2010.
Photo: US Coast Guard. © picture alliance/dpa/US Coast Guard.

p. 34

Still from BP's underwater "spillcam," a live video
feed documenting attempts to curb the flow of crude oil at the
site of the leak, Deepwater Horizon, Gulf of
Mexico, July 10, 2010. © picture alliance/dpa/BP File.

Chapter Three

p. 41

sHell No! protesters demonstrate against Royal Dutch Shell's
Polar Pioneer drilling rig, near Seattle, May 16, 2015.
Photo: David Ryder. © David Ryder/Getty Images.

p. 46
The Pacific Climate Warriors, activists from the Pacific Islands,
form a flotilla to blockade the entrance to the world's
largest coal port, Newcastle, Australia, October 17, 2014.
Photo: David Gray. © David Gray/Reuters.

p. 53
David Dodge, Syncrude oil-sands mining operations with
upgrader plant in the background, Alberta, Canada, 2007.
Courtesy of David Dodge, Pembina.org.

Chapter Four
pp. 62–63
Edward Burtynsky, *Oil Fields #19ab, Belridge, California,
USA*, 2003. Courtesy of Nicholas Metivier Gallery, Toronto/
Galerie Springer, Berlin. © Edward Burtynsky.

p. 64
Edward Burtynsky, *Oil Fields #27, Bakersfield, California, USA*,
2004. Courtesy of Nicholas Metivier Gallery, Toronto/
Galerie Springer, Berlin. © Edward Burtynsky.

pp. 66–67
Louis Helbig, *Effluent Steam (Tu ch'ele t'ok'é heli) (nipiy kā pe
sākicowak piwāpiskohk ohci sīpīsis)*, +57° 14' 0.59", -111° 33' 10.50,
Muskeg River Mine, Fort McKay, Alberta, Canada, 2012.
Courtesy of Louis Helbig, beautifuldestruction.ca.

pp. 72–73
Richard Misrach, *Abandoned Trailer, Mississippi River, near Dow Chemical Plant, Plaquemine, Louisiana*, 1998. Courtesy of Fraenkel Gallery, San Francisco; Pace/MacGill Gallery, New York; and Marc Selwyn Fine Art, Los Angeles. © Richard Misrach.

pp. 74–75
SCAPE Landscape Architecture, *Petrochemical Landscape*, 2012. Digital map from *Petrochemical America* (New York: Aperture, 2012). Courtesy of SCAPE Landscape Architecture.

pp. 76–77
SCAPE Landscape Architecture, *Requiem for a Bayou*, 2012. Photomontage from *Petrochemical America* (New York: Aperture, 2012). Courtesy of SCAPE Landscape Architecture.

pp. 82–83
Armin Linke, *Museum of Evolution of Life*, Chandigarh, India, 2014. Courtesy of Armin Linke.

Chapter Five

p. 92
Elizabeth Stephens and Annie Sprinkle with Daniel Wasko Design, banner from the website *SexEcology*, accessed February 2017. http://www.sexecology.org. Courtesy of the artists.

p. 94
Pony Express (Ian Sinclair and Loren Kronemyer), *Ecosexual Bathhouse*, Next Wave Festival, Melbourne, 2015. Image: Sarah Walker. Courtesy of the artists.

p. 98
Bolivian demonstration to support the Law of the
Rights of Mother Earth, at the Peoples' World Conference
on Climate Change and the Rights of Mother Earth in
Cochabamba, Bolivia, April 19–22, 2010.
Courtesy of the Indigenous Environmental Network.

pp. 100–101
Ursula Biemann and Paulo Tavares, *Forest Law*, 2014. Synchro-
nized video projection, 42 min., assemblage of documents, artist
book. Installation view, BAK, Utrecht. Courtesy of the artists.

p. 104
History of Others, *The Trial*, 2014. History of Others is a
collaboration between artist Terike Haapoja and writer Laura
Gustafsson. Photo: Saara Hannula. Courtesy of the artists.

p. 106
Screenshot of the website *Climate Games*, accessed December
2015. https://www.climategames.net (site currently unavailable).

p. 110
An international artist-activist coalition stages the event
"Big Oil Out of Culture" in front of the Musée du Louvre,
Paris, December 9, 2015. Photo: Sumugan Sivanesan.
Courtesy of Sumugan Sivanesan.

T. J. Demos is a professor in the History of Art and Visual Culture Department, University of California, Santa Cruz, and founder and director of its Center for Creative Ecologies. He writes widely on the intersection of contemporary art, global politics, and ecology, and is the author of several books, including: *Decolonizing Nature: Contemporary Art and the Politics of Ecology* (Sternberg Press, 2016); *The Migrant Image: The Art and Politics of Documentary During Global Crisis* (Duke University Press, 2013, winner of the College Art Association's 2014 Frank Jewett Mather Award); and *Return to the Postcolony: Specters of Colonialism in Contemporary Art* (Sternberg Press, 2013).

T. J. Demos
Against the Anthropocene
Visual Culture and Environment Today

Published by Sternberg Press

Copyediting: Marnie Slater
Proofreading: Mark Soo
Image research: Louisa Nyman, Isabella Ritchie
Printing: KOPA, Lithuania
Design: Miriam Rech, Berlin

Cover image: Still from Globaïa's video *Welcome to the Anthropocene*, 2012.
http://anthropocene.info/short-films.php. Courtesy of Félix Pharand-Deschênes/Globaïa.

ISBN 978-3-95679-210-6

Sternberg Press
Caroline Schneider
Karl-Marx-Allee 78
D-10243 Berlin
www.sternberg-press.com